12-2

D0846529

A Beer Drinker's
GUIDE
to
SOUTHERN
GERMANY

JAMES D. ROBERTSON

*This is dedicated to the
past, present and future brewmasters of Germany
for holding true to the great tradition.*

All inquiries should be addressed to Bosak Publishing Company, 4764 Galicia Way, Oceanside, CA 92056, (619) 724-4447.

ISBN: 0-9635332-3-1

Printed in the United States of America

About the Author

James D. Robertson is a retired electronics engineer, having worked for the Department of the Army and the Department of Defense for thirty-four years following his graduation from MIT in 1956. Worldwide travel associated with his career exposed him to much of the world's bounty, and he discovered that he had a taste for it all. Most important, he felt a need to bring the appreciation of food, wine, and beer to others.

When at home, he wrote about wine, beer, food, and restaurants. He has been published over 200 times in fifteen publications, including *Cosmopolitan* and *Consumer's Digest*. To date, he has written five books: *The Great American Beer Book* and three editions of *The Connoisseurs Guide to Beer*, and *The Beer Log*. This guide brings that total to six.

He attributes his tasting talent to an extraordinary palate memory, which was honed to a sharp edge in many years of wine tasting. In those days of wine discovery (1960s and 1970s), parlor games included naming the exact growers and vintages of a selection of wines. The talent developed at that time carried through into the world of beer.

Since retirement in 1990, he has traveled across the United States and Canada several times, and visited many countries in Europe and the Orient, tasting beer. He plans to continue the effort to hunt down all the beers of the world.

Contents

Preface

During my thirty four years as an electronic engineer, I frequently travelled to Germany. It was my initial extended visit during the winter of 1961 that expanded my mind to the potential of beer. Even though my childhood was spent during a time when Germany was the world's great villain, I came to love the country, its people, its food, its wine and its beer. The only problem I ever had in Deutschland was that I was working and never had enough time to frolic about the countryside enjoying the great food, wine and brew. Despite that and because I was there over fifteen different times, I did manage to see most of the historic sites and beauty spots, eat in most of the great and famous restaurants and taste over 700 beers. Still, there was always the thought of "doing a number" on Germany; a trip solely aimed at tasting the world famous German brews while enjoying the marvelous cuisine — and doing it with a passion, in other words, to go on a beer pilgrimage to Germany.

This guide is done in the form of such a pilgrimage. It reports on hundreds of beers available to taste that are not exported, provides tips on where to find beer, brewery restaurants, brewery guesthouses (*gasthaus*), brew-pubs (*hausbrauereien*), drink markets (*getränkemarkt*) and gives all the beer related information that travel agents don't know enough to tell you. So, sit yourself down in the car (for that is the only way to reach the little out-of-the-way places where they have been brewing beer for centuries), lean back and think of German beer.

The centerpiece of this guide is indeed that pilgrimage made in 1991 by two beer lovers solely for the purpose of enjoying fine cuisine and tasting beer. It does, however, contain material from previous visits (especially the last three business trips taken prior to my retirement), so in essence, to do what we show in these three weeks would take more like a month to accomplish. We did maintain a pace of at least 20 new beers tasted each day, most of them in our hotel room at night so we wouldn't have to face a highway in an impaired condition. German police will tolerate impaired pedestrians, but the legal limit on blood alcohol while operating a motor vehicle is .08%.

Off To A Fast Start

On arrival in Frankfurt, the most likely arrival point in Germany, we picked up our rental car, figured out how to get it into reverse, backed out of the stall and headed off south on the autobahn toward Stuttgart. My travelling companion was Bill Geiger of Middletown, NJ. Bill is a perfect companion on a beer pilgrimage. He has a great palate for fine food and a prodigious thirst for fine German beer. In driving around Germany looking for beer you need at least two people — a driver and a navigator who can successfully wrestle with those ungainly European maps. When you find the beer, it also helps to have enough people to do justice to the task of dispatching large quantities of brew without attracting undue attention, not that that is much of a problem in Germany.

Heading south from Frankfurt, the land is fairly flat. The hills of the Odenwald are not far away to the east and their presence is comforting because I know how many good brews are made over in the little towns of that area. To the west is the Rheinhessen with its magnificent wines, but while we may taste a wine or two before we are done, beer is our quest on this trip.

It is late morning and our immediate destination is Pfungstadt and Bruno Maruhn's famous "Der Grosste Biermarkt Der Welt." The World's Greatest Beer Market is located just west of the #5 autobahn in Pfungstadt, not far fom the Darmstadter Kreuz, an autobahn crossover. There is nothing like it anywhere else. For many years the store claimed to offer 943 different brews. I had told Herr Maruhn's son that the figure was overly modest. They now advertise 2,225 brands, a number which I believe to be somewhat exaggerated. The correct number lies between the two, although it may reach that higher figure before too long. Certainly, the effect on a beer lover is overwhelming. There is a tendency

to wander the aisles aimlessly just taking it all in. Hundreds of beers lined on long shelves, aisle after aisle of them. Also there are beer paraphernalia, signs, glasses and the like for sale. There are also liquors, snacks, fruit and soft drinks. Our purpose was to load the trunk of our car with Doppelbocks, Maibocks, Oktoberfestbier, Märzenbier, Weizenbock and other rare birds that are hard to find, even in the towns where they are made. Most of these specialty brews are made in small quantity and disappear soon after release. They can be found in Pfungstadt long after they are only a memory elsewhere. We were to be in Germany about 18 days and in planning out the trip in advance, we figured that we could reasonably sample about 20 beers each day. Except for a few treasured items we might find, our goal was to taste only ones new to us. We had stopped at this fabled store only to find the odd special item and to allow a measure of insurance to get us over those days when we might find little or nothing (that day never did come).

Maruhn's "Der Grosste Biermarkt Der Welt" in Pfungstadt.

This stop also gave us the opportunity to taste the local brews. **Privatbrauerei Hildebrand Gmbh. & Co., K.G. Pfungstädter Brauerei** offers **PFUNGSTÄDTER** — pale yellow-gold, hop and sour malt aroma, good flavor with a touch of roasted malt to give it richness, good tasting finish, good balance, long malt aftertaste; **BOCKALE PREMIUM CLASS** — pale gold, faint hop and roasted malt aroma, highly carbonated, big hop flavor and long hop aftertaste, could use more malt for a better balance; **ST. NIKOLAUS DUNKLES STARKBIER** — copper-amber, caramel and roasted malt nose, delicious and appetizing, palate is big malt right from the start and it stays, a little smoky-toasty, faint sour hops join the malt in the long aftertaste, very attractive Christmas beer and **PFUNGSTÄDTER MAIBOCK** — pale amber, lovely malt nose, hop flavor, well-balanced with malt, long dry hop aftertaste, a very nice appetizing May Bock. Nearby Darmstadt has some excellent beers. One of the best comes from **Privatbrauerei W. Rummel.** It is **DARMSTADTER UR BOCK DOPPELBOCK** — amber, light malt nose, good malt flavor, finely carbonated, there is some complexity contributed by background hops, good body, hops show best in the finish and aftertaste, very well-balanced, very long dry hop and malt aftertaste. The others we found were from **Brauerei Grohe** and were **GROHE BOCK** — amber, lovely fresh fruity malt aroma, beautiful off-dry malt and hop flavor, excellent balance, medium to light body, dry hop finish, long off-dry malt aftertaste, a very pleasant easy-to-drink brew and **GROHE MÄRZEN** — amber, fruity-malt nose, flowery fruit-like off-dry malt flavor, touch of banana, light to medium body, medium to long off-dry malt aftertaste.

When in Darmstadt, you might notice that most of the buildings seem relatively new. They pretty much date back only to 1944 when the city was reduced to rubble in an incendiary raid. There are some excellent restorations and the Landesmuseum with its collection of German primitives, porcelain museum and artists' colony are there for your diversion. There is even the Wella Museum of hair and beauty care. If you are staying nearby you might visit the **Kronenbräugarten** to try some local beer. It is on the corner of Dieburgerstrasse and Spessart Ring.

Having selected our three dozen treasures to fill evenings of days when we might find little of interest (or to take home if we don't get around to tasting them en route), we headed south out of the Darmstadt-Pfungstadt area. It was now time for lunch which, in Germany, is the main meal of the day. Remembering a good dining experience in Weinheim, a mid-sized town just off the autobahn, we sought out a bistro associated with a wine import house. As a choice for lunch this day, however, it was unsuitable, now being open only for dinner (an unusual occurrence in Germany that indicates a substantial local American population). Mildly disappointed, I drove further down the street looking for a promising alternative.

Bill Geiger spotted it first. The **Woinemer Hausbrauerei**, a brewpub that first opened for business in 1986, looked like just the thing for two hungry pilgrims looking for their first culinary/beer experience. There were tables outdoors in a covered courtyard and several dining/drinking rooms inside. It was a bit cool outside so we opted to eat in the room with the bar where one can watch the beer being pulled. This also puts you in view of the interior windows overlooking the brewplant.

We were careful to avoid sitting at the *Stammtisch,* a table set aside for the regulars. This table is usually a bit larger than the other tables and frequently adorned with a reserved sign. It is not for the use of the general public, but rather is reserved for the town fathers, family, or just the regular patrons who have earned special dispensation. An "outsider" can sit at the *Stammtisch* only by invitation and it is considered to be quite an honor. Other than the restricted *Stammtisch,* you may sit at any table that has an opening, even if already partially occupied. You don't have to engage the other patrons in conversation, but it is an excellent opportunity to meet the locals. Some of my fondest memories of Germany and much valued information came from such meetings. If a table is not covered with a cloth, it may be a self service table, an old tradition that goes back centuries and allows patrons to bring their own food to a watering hole. You will certainly see that practice in action at the Kloster Andechs, where the older citizens of the town trudge up the hill with their lunch bags to enjoy the excellent beer. Remember, when the waiter comes to take your order, be prepared to give it to him. They will quickly flit away to do other work if they think you are not ready. There are some traditional beer gardens where you are expected to find you own mug, wash it and take it to the tap to be filled.

The Woinemer menu ranged from *hausgemakt* (homemade) soups to hefty veal and pork entrées typical of the region. As we were still in the process of recovering from many hours of eating airline food, we chose

Woinemer Hausbrauerei in Weinheim.

the *Ungärische gulaschsuppe* (Hungarian goulasch) and dark brown bread to help sample the beers. Goulasch in Germany varies widely with the establishment. It seems like every kitchen has its unique recipe. All are good; some are spectacular. Also most times the bread is made on premises and can be a treat. Remember, if the menu doesn't say that bread comes with the meal you order, they don't automatically bring it to the table. It has to be ordered like any other menu item and will appear on your bill. This goulasch was splendid and the bread was equal to it. So were the beers.

Ordering food and beer in Germany is probably the best reason to learn a little of the language. A good dictionary will give you the words. Every syllable of every word is enunciated. There are few silent consonants and most of those are obvious. A most worthwhile sentence to use is *"Ich möchte gern _____ haben, bitte.* with a noun filling the blank. Pronounced more or less Ish mershte gairn _____ha-ben, bit-te, it says I would like to have _____, please. That phrase has been my opening for getting anything from a toothpick to a room for the night. Although not incorrect to sit down at a bar or table and simply say "Bier, bitte," it is fairly imprecise. Better to order a Pils (peelse), Export, Weizen Kristallklar, Hefe-Weizen, or a trade name brew to save the waitress asking which kind of beer it is that you want. Remember, the Germans are very precise people.

WOINEMER HELL was a hazy amber brew with a thick head, bright hop aroma and flavor and a long aftertaste with plenty of both hops and malt. It was richly flavored and perfectly balanced. **WOINEMER MAI BOCK** looked like the Hell to the eye, but the nose was fairly faint in both malt and hops. The flavor was surprisingly big and straight malt, as one would expect from a May bock. A big bodied brew, it remained malty until the finish when the hops came in with strength and stayed through the long aftertaste. The only disappointment was **WOINEMER DUNKEL**, a dark amber-brown brew with a soft malt aroma and flavor, medium body and short malt aftertaste. It was a surprising letdown after the first two, but probably suffered from the comparison.

Woinemer also offered a *Bierbrand*, a brandy made from beer. These malt based brandies are not common in Germany. They are most likely to come from central and northern regions. I have never seen Bierbrand in Bavaria, they preferring to make other kinds of brandy from grapes, fruit, honey and spices. Mention Bierbrand to a Bavarian and he is likely to ask you where you saw such a thing. Tell him and he will say "Yes, *they* would make something like that up there." This Bierbrand was very interesting, with its malt origins only faintly evident. It was clean and bright, very different from other brandies and quite good.

Driving out of Weinheim, I pointed out to my companion that all but restaurants were closed. In small towns and even in big cities, shops close for a two hour lunch. It is their big meal of the day and everybody breaks for it. There are very few exceptions. In recent years, a few shops, mostly grocery stores, stay open during lunch. Virtually everybody goes to lunch and they are leisurely about it. If you plan to do shopping in Germany, be advised that most stores close for the day by 6-6:30pm. I understand that these short hours (remember, they were closed for a couple of hours during the lunch break) are due to a law passed over 40 years ago curtailing business hours to counter the German's tendency to work until he drops.

Another useful tip about restaurants is tipping. Your bill will contain a service charge, usually 10%. This is to pay your waiter. You aren't expected to tip further unless some extraordinary service is provided, although small coins (pfennigs) are usually left on the table as added gratuity. Also, the waiter is responsible for collecting the tab. If they don't, for any reason, it comes out of their pay. When you call for *"Die Rechnung, bitte."* (The reckoning, please.) or *"Zahlen, bitte."* (Check, please.), the waiter expects you to pay them and they will make change. A cash register at the exit is an unusual sight in Germany, although it has begun to appear.

A note to gentlemen: Do not be surprised if the cleaning lady for a toilet is present within sight of the urinal. She has no interest in you and has seen thousands go to that wall. Your only concern should be to have a few pfennigs to put into the plate, which is to pay her for the paper towel to dry your hands and for keeping the place clean.

Back on the autobahn, we continued our southward trek to Stuttgart. The plan was to spend four nights in the Stuttgart area. It was not that Stuttgart is particularly exciting for beer lovers, but the territory is a good central location to use as a temporary base. From there you may radiate out into Baden-Wurttemberg, Schwabia and the Schwarzwald without having to pack up each morning. The down side was that Stuttgart is an industrial center and hotel rates are higher than in the countryside. On our travels in the area, we did find better places that we would stay in during future visits. These will be identified later. Stuttgart itself had its beginnings as a stud farm or *Stutengarten* about 1000 years ago. It became a center for farmers to bring their crops and animals for sale and still serves that function, with early Saturday morning markets attracting farmers and their wares from miles around. Modern Stuttgart is also the home of booming industry, the most famous of which are Daimler-Benz, Porsche and Robert Bosch. There is an excellent downtown mall with many modern shops, a city center with cathedrals, churches, ancient fortress remains, museums and art galleries. The Staatsgalerie is world famous for its collection of paintings. If you prefer, or are an automobile buff, you can visit the Daimler-Benz museum (which is sure to have your favorite Mercedes) and the Porsche Museum, both of which are free. You can even visit the Porschewerk, where you can wander about at will or go on a guided tour of the production facility.

Settled in at our digs in Vaihingen-Stuttgart at the Hotel Restaurant Römerhof at Robert Leicht Strasse 93, near the Robert Leicht Brauerei and the Patch Barracks, once HQ for Rommel's Panzerkorps and present location of one of the many U.S. military bases in the area, we wandered downtown in search of beer. In Vaihingen, there is an excellent brewery restaurant at **Robert Leicht A.G.** that features a full menu of moderately priced continental and German entrees. Naturally, they serve only the Robert Leicht beers. **SCHWABEN BRÄU PILSENER** is found everywhere in Vaihingen on draft. This golden brew has a hop nose and taste, medium to good body and a long dry hop aftertaste. It is a good pils, but among German pils type brews, just average. In bottle, you are likely to find **SCHWABEN BRÄU MEISTER PILS** which may be the same beer only packaged. It is bright gold, with a hop nose, pronounced hop flavor, hop finish and long dry hop aftertaste. The **SCHWABEN BRÄU EXPORT** is the "export" style equivalent, having a bit more malt, more alcohol and an overall smoother nature than the pils. It is bright tawny-gold, with a balanced hop and malt nose and flavor, good body, fairly smooth, appetizing, long dry malt and hop aftertaste. Mostly, I prefer the more hoppy pils beers of a brewery. In the case of Robert Leicht, I find the export more appealing. **DAS ECHTE SCHWABEN BRÄU** is a recent (late 1980s) offering that has a greater density (13 vs. 12 degrees for their other beers). It is tawny-gold, has a big hop nose, heavy body, big hop flavor with plenty of malt in support and a long dry hop aftertaste. They also offer **SCHWABEN BRÄU URTYP 1878**, a golden brew with a dry hop nose and flavor. It is very dry and lacks complexity.

Since it was our first night in Germany and our internal clocks were still awry, we decided to go down to Stuttgart city and wander around. We had heard of a brewpub in the downtown mall district. I thought that would be a nice final touch for our opening day and, failing that, we could always enjoy some Dinkelacker, Stuttgarter Hofbrau or Sanwald wheat beers (now made by Dinkelacker). We left the car in one of the peripheral parking areas at the large downtown mall that covers what used to be several blocks of downtown streets and walked to the **Stuttgarter Lokalbrauerei** at 31 Calwer Strasse. It was an upstairs bar jammed with young well-dressed patrons, Stuttgart's yuppie population. Totally unlike any other pub I've visited in Germany, every eye turned to us as we entered; obviously the place to see and be seen by that social set. We laced our way through the press of people to a couple of seats at the back of the bar near the waitress station. As we did so, we noticed that there was a large variety of foods available, everything from wursts to salads and vegetables, from snacks to full meal service. There were two brews available. We started with the **CALWER-ECK-BRÄU NATURTRUB.** It was cloudy gold, had a yeasty hop aroma, good and interesting flavor with yeast, hops and malt and a dry finish and aftertaste. The flavor was a bit off-dry in front, but became drier as it crossed the palate to end quite dry. It was smooth without any roughness. The word "*naturtrub*" means that the yeast has not been filtered out. It works very well for this beer. They also had **FLORIANO MAIBOCK**, a cloudy brown brew with a thick brown head. It had a very faint malt aroma, a smooth malt palate that was slightly sweet up front, but dry at the finish and into the long aftertaste. Both beers were excellent.

Some other pleasant dining I have enjoyed in Stuttgart is at the Stuttgarter Ratskeller on Hirsch Strasse in the downtown mall area. One of my favorites there is a kirschsteak, beefsteak panfried in black cherries and mustard and served with pistachios and rice. They also have an excellent Hungarian goulash and an interesting *Schneckensuppe* (snail soup). There is also a good line of local wines and the beer of Stuttgarter Hofbrau. Another restaurant is the Schellenturm at Weberstrasse 72, on the edge of the downtown mall area, built in an old prison tower, but which today offers cozy dining on several levels, featuring fine wines and Dinkelacker beer. Outside of Stuttgart, in the *naturpark* behind Vaihingen just off the autobahn between Vaihingen and Leonberg are two places worth remembering. One is the Waldhotel Schatten, which has two excellent (though moderately expensive) restaurants and the Hotel Waldgasthaus Glemstal which has very quiet rooms (except for Sunday morning when the target range in back may be active) and a restaurant which specializes in wild game dinners like exotic venison dishes, trout from their own tank (there is a hatchery about a mile down the road) and various game birds. The old Sanwald Brewery Gasthof on Silberburg Str. still has the Sanwald wheat beers. The best place to taste the Dinkelacker beers is the brewery/restaurant in front of the brew-plant on Tübinger Str. I have heard of another brew-pub out in a town adjacent to the airport, but failed to find it in several attempts.

One thing to remember about Stuttgart is that in Bad Canstatt, a suburb just across the Neckar River, there is a Volkfest held for 16 days in September-October. The second biggest beer festival in the world, this Bad Canstatter Volkfest is a huge carnival, similar to Munich's Oktoberfest, but smaller. It is a lot of fun, however and the local breweries make special Oktoberfest beer for it and each operates a festhalle.

Schwäbia and The Schwarzwalder

South of Stuttgart is a mountainous area called the Schwäbische Alb. It is a beautiful area with lots of farmland and forests that has been inhabited for many centuries. Buildings dating to the 15th century can be found in most towns and relics going back another 200-300 years can be seen in local museums. Feudal castles and bergs dot the high grounds with their commanding aspects. The famous Hohenzollernschloss is in Hechingen. Lichtenstein's berg is the top end of a cliff that towers over the town. Sigmaringen Castle is a fascinating tour with its collection of feudal weaponry. Centuries old towns and cities of the region are treasures to walk with images of old Germany everywhere. This can be particularly interesting to Americans whose cultural heritage goes back only to the 17th century.

Our adventure in Schwäbia began with a drive down the #81 Autobahn toward Singen. Autobahns are incredibly fast ways to get between points on the map if you don't care to see much in the way of scenery or historical sights. Strangely enough, you can buy beer (and even hard liquor) at rest stops. There are many stretches in rural areas where there is no speed limit except for minimums in certain lanes. In more populated areas, speed limits are appearing as the number of cars on the roads increase, but these are on the order of 100-120 km/hr (to convert kilometers to miles multiply by 0.6). After about a half hour, we quit the speedway and wandered over to Tübingen (to shop some beer stores) and then down to the spectacular Burg Hohenzollern, ancestral home of the Hohenzollerns who ruled Germany before confederation. The fortress sits atop a small mountain looking like a classical medieval castle. It absolutely dominates the landscape and can be seen for many

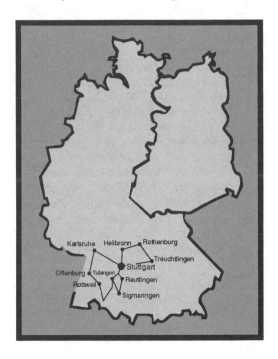

miles from the plain it overlooks. It is also open to tourists. Tübingen is of great interest, as well. It is a city dominated by its famous University that was founded over 500 years ago. While I can't name you specific buildings of interest, a walking tour of the town is a distinct pleasure. It has the serenity of a college town and, not having suffered the ravages of WW II, the buildings represent the architecture of over 400 years and are connected by a maze of twisting and turning streets and alleys.

At lunch time we reached Sigmaringen and spotted the **Brauerei Zoller-Hof** which has a marvelous *Gäststette* (guest-restaurant) tacked on the front end of the brewery — a sort of 150 year old brew-pub. To our delight the menu featured Schwäbian country specialties such as multarschen — a sort of ravioli stuffed with meats and vegetables. There were also traditional Schwäbian country style sausages and meat dishes. An extensive beer menu offered all of the brewery's seasonal products, many of them on draft and all of them in bottles. When we explained to the waitress that we wanted to try one of everything, she became most interested in our motives. We struggled with our language skills until she remarked "*Bier Probe,*" meaning a beer testing, tasting or sampling. She then went into the back of the bar and brought out some items that weren't listed on the card for our tasting.

Brauerei Gaststätte Zoller-Hof in Sigmaringen.

The first beer tried was **ZOLLER FURSTEN PILS**, a pale gold pils with a big thick head that lasted to the bottom of the glass (ah, how nice to have the head of an all malt beer), light hop aroma, dry hop flavor, dry hop finish and a very long dry hop aftertaste. **ZOLLER SPECIAL EXPORT** was similar to the pils except that there was more malt on the palate and the aftertaste had some malty sweetness balanced in behind the hops. It is an excellent "export" style. **ZOLLER DUNKLES BOCKLE BOCKBIER** was an amber brew with a thick tan head, faint malt aroma, rich dry malt flavor and great length. **ZOLLER FIDELIS WEIZEN** was cloudy brown, with a rich and spicy malt nose and big creamy, spicy malt flavor. This is a dark hefe-weizen that goes beyond mere refreshment. **ZOLLER BRENZKOFER DUNKEL** was an amber beer with a light hop aroma and a dry malt flavor that was a bit short. **ZOLLER FURSTEN KRISTALL WEIZEN** was light and refreshing with a nice wheaty malt character. **ZOLLER FURSTEN HEFE-WEIZEN** was cloudy gold, had a great clove spice aroma, creamy texture, clean spicy clove and malt flavor, excellent balance and a long, clean, spicy-malty-fruity aftertaste. A wonderful bright and refreshing hefe-weizen. The folks at the Zoller were most accommodating. They were sincerely sorry that the brewmaster was away on that day, else he would have taken us on a tour of the brewery. This brings up the question of anonymity. If you announce that you are a devotée of beer, there is a chance that you will get a tour of the brewery. The German brewers are enthusiastic and even ordinary tourists professing a great love of beer might well be treated as visiting dignitaries. As pleasureful as it might be, it could consume a lot of time and each traveller will have to decide how much of a day can be allotted to unexpected tours.

This was our first encounter with weizenbier or wheat beer and it was a good one. The hefe-weizen are expected to be cloudy with yeast since it is not filtered out. I find they have much more flavor and are more satisfying. The Kristall-Klar (crystal clear) have the yeast filtered out and, while still good tasting, are more like a pils/helles. You will find you gravitate to one or the other as your preference.

To help you walk off the beer is Sigmaringen's Schloss, another turreted Romantic castle that will eat up some film. To me the highlight was the collection of arms and armor, well worth the price of admission.

Near Sigmaringen, about 6 km away in the town of Bingen, is **Privater Brauerei-Gasthof Zum Lamm.** This brewery guesthouse is well off the beaten track and doesn't even appear except on the best of maps. There are only four rooms, but the *spiesekarte* (menu) features Schwäbian specialties, excellent beer and a *bierhefebrand* (beer yeast brandy). These brewery guest houses offer excellent and reasonable accommodations, especially when you can sit down for a fine evening meal with their house brewed beer and stay there for the night. We arrived there on the Lamm's *ruhetag* (their day of rest and therefore closed), but luckily found their brews across the street at a small grocery store. **LAMM BRÄU PILSENER** was a beautiful bright golden beer with a finely balanced malt and hop aroma, a good hop flavor well balanced with malt and a complex long dry hop aftertaste. As good as was the pils, the **LAMM BRÄU EDEL HELL** was even better with its bright hop aroma and flavor beautifully backed with an abundance of malt and finishing up with a dry hop aftertaste. A pair of excellent beers that we could not find more than 4 km from the source.

Privater Brauerei-Gasthof Zum Lamm in Bingen, near Sigmaringen.

Some other beers of the area found in shops were one from **Zwiefalter Klosterbrauerei** in the recuperative health resort of Zwiefalter: **ZWIE-FALTER KLOSTERBRÄU PILSNER EDELTYP**, a golden brew with a faintly roasted malt aroma, malt flavor with good hop support, a big lusty flavor, good body and a long dry malt and hop aftertaste; and one from Wilhermsdorf (nearer to Ravensburg) made by **Brauhaus Wilhermsdorf: ALT WILHERMSDORFER DUNKEL**, a very deep amber brew with a smooth dry malt aroma, dry malt palate, off-dry malt finish, back taste of alcohol exists despite a low alcohol rating (4.1%), soft texture, long malt aftertaste, a good flavor that grows on you.

Another bright spot in the Schwäbian Alb is the little town of Trochtelfingen (located on the road between Sigmaringen and Reutlingen). This picturesque village seems to have been frozen in time for several hundred years and beautifully kept in the style. One of its attractions is the **Albquell Brauhaus**, a relative newcomer to town, having been founded only about 150 years ago. This is another private brewery guest house with rooms, a menu featuring Schwäbian cuisine and a number of fine beers. The town, especially the Albquell, is most attractive and I plan to spend some time here on future visits. **ALBQUELL PILSNER** was solid hops from start to finish, but carefully ministered and expertly balanced. **ALBQUELL URTRUNK** was similar, but much bigger and better flavored. **ALBQUELL EDELBIER EXPORT** was again similar, but had more malt, an even better balance, bigger body and great length. It finished drier than the others despite the increased malt. All three were very well made brews.

Albquell Brauhaus in Trochtelfingen.

Near to Stuttgart is another interesting small town named Sindelfingen. It has a downtown center section with 500 year old buildings, but is generally made up of modern offices and factories dating back only to the postwar boom years in Germany ('70s and '80s). There are a few fine restaurants in town offering Schwäbian specialties (hard to find in the more cosmopolitan Stuttgart), some lively nightspots and another **Brauerei Lamm.** Since Germany was originally a collection of feudal states, many businesses dating back to a time before the federation have the same name. As Lamm beer from Sindelfingen wouldn't be offered in Bingen and Bingen's Lamm would never be seen in Sindelfingen, it doesn't matter much and arguments for one or the other are likely to be moot. The Lamm beers have always been pleasant, light and refreshing well-made brews greatly favored by the towns' residents. One of my favorite places in Sindelfingen to enjoy a quiet supper is at the Holzkiste restaurant on Vaihinger Strasse. They occasionally will have wild game dishes and always have Schwäbian specialties and very good *Schnitzel* (pork and veal cutlets) and, of course, the local beer. **LAMM BRÄU PILS** is brilliant gold, has a beautiful hop nose and bright hop flavor, bitter hop finish, long bitter hop aftertaste and is a very good serviceable beer, especially with food. **LAMM BRÄU EXPORT** is brilliant amber, has a balanced hop-malt aroma and taste, is smooth and appetizing. Malt dominates the mid-palate, hops in lead in front and at finish and there is a long dry hop and malt aftertaste. It is another good beer with food. The newest product from Lamm is **WURTTEMBERG'S NATURTRUBE LAMM BRÄU**, a golden, highly carbonated (unusual for Germany) brew with little aroma, but with a big complex rich dry malt and hop flavor, dry hop finish and a medium long dry malt aftertaste. Overall, it is a very fine effort.

An interesting watering hole in Sindelfingen is a restaurant/tavern named Funzel. It is crowded, smoky (Germans smoke too much) and loud. It also has a great beer list that includes Andechs Doppelbock, the beers from Kaltenberg, local beer and a number of popular beers from the north of Germany. I always stop by there when in the area for a "nightcap" or two or three, naturally ending up with some Andechs, my most favorite beer of them all. We will discuss Andechs at great length later while in Bavaria.

Being in the Stuttgart area, we sought out what might be new or different from that city and environs. We did not wish to gather up any of the familiar items exported regularly to the U.S. There are more brews than are humanly possible to handle in a short visit without adding on those we have already tasted. One of the big breweries in Stuttgart well-known to Americans is **Dinkelacker Wulle, A.G.** and we found that, much to our surprise, most Dinkelacker brews are found stateside. Two notable exceptions are: **DINKELACKER WEIHNACHTSBIER SPEZIAL** (Christmas Beer) — deep gold, very nice hop and toasted malt nose, beautifully balanced malt and hop flavor, good body, long malt aftertaste ends dry hops very late, a delicious satisfying beer; and **DINKELACKER VOLKSFESTBIER** — brilliant gold, big dense head, huge hop nose, good body, big appetizing malt and hop flavor, clean and dry, long dry hop aftertaste, this seems to be available only at the Bad Canstatter Volksfest near Stuttgart. Another brewery in the area which does not export beer is **Stuttgarter Hofbrau** which offers **STUTTGARTER HOFBRAU HERRN PILS** — bright gold, aroma of wet wool, hop flavor, plenty of supporting malt, slightly sour hop finish, long dry hop aftertaste; **STUTTGARTER HOFBRAU PILSNER** — slightly tawny-gold, good hop nose is sort of sweet, austere dry hop palate, good body, long dry hop aftertaste; and **STUTTGARTER HOFBRAU WEIHNACHTS-BIER** — pale gold, strange offish nose, dull flavor that isn't particularly like hops or malt, uninteresting, medium long aftertaste like the flavor. A former weissbier brewery in the area was the **Sanwald Brauerei**. The beers are now made by Dinkelacker and they still offer **SANWALD WEIZEN DUNKEL HEFETRUB** — tawny-amber, big head, clean wheaty-malt nose, bright clean flavor is mostly wheat and malt with just a touch of lactic character, taste is just a little bit sweet, good balance between the sweetness and the lactic bite, long dry aftertaste; **SANWALD WEIZEN KRONE KRISTALLKLAR** — bright gold, big head, faint wheaty-malt nose is on the sweet side, light flavor is also slightly sweet like the nose, acid is way in back, almost unnoticeable, light body, long off-dry malt aftertaste with lactic spice appearing at the end, drinkable but not much offered; **SANWALD HEFE WEISSE** — bright gold, huge head, faint fruity-tart nose, light dry malt flavor with very little acidic tang, pleasant but brief; and **SANWALD WEIZEN PERLSTARK** — bright gold, clean weizen (wheat -malt - lactic) nose, not much lactic spice, smooth, well-balanced, slightly sour aftertaste. I have never seen these beers far from Stuttgart.

The following day was one of the many German religious holidays. There are more than a dozen of these spread out across the year and always come as a surprise to tourists. There are no stores open. No grocery stores, no getränkemarkts, no breweries. In certain areas even restaurants may not be open or are operating with reduced hours as there may be special services or celebrations that everyone is expected to attend. This failing of openness should only slow a quest for beer. Local beers (and some more distant ones as well) can still be found at gas stations which are open. The beer costs more, but is available. We drove again into Schwäbia headed for the Schwarzwalder (Black Forest) stopping at gas stations and picking up many of the local brands.

It is worth comment on where one finds beer in Germany and what factors are involved. First of all, if there is a brewery in town, their beer can be found everywhere beer is sold. Those labels may be the only ones you will find. This will be the situation for a radius of several miles. For instance, the Robert Leicht brewery is in Vaihingen, a suburb of Stuttgart. At all the restaurants and gasthaus bars in town, you will find Robert Leicht brands and an occasional beer from Dinkelacker or one of the other Stuttgart breweries. If you wish to try the Stuttgart beers, however, you had best go look in the city for them, for even though Vaihingen is less than five miles from the downtown, the brews don't wander far from the brewery. Only a half dozen kilometers away in Sindelfingen, you would be hard pressed to find a Schwäben Bräu, for Lamm Bräu is brewed there. All the restaurants and gasthaus bars will serve that local beer. This makes it difficult to find the brands of the small breweries as you must go directly to the source. There are, of course, exceptions to the rule, but they are few and far between. A beer may occasionally pop up many miles from its home, but there are usually special circumstances and it doesn't happen often.

Beer is the least expensive in grocery stores. Even small neighborhood stores will carry one or two labels, usually the local beer. Supermarkets (which have become common only in the last decade or so) may have a dozen or more brands, most from nearby breweries and a select few from some far away brewer. Prices range from 65 pfennig (40 cents) to 1.5 Deutschmarks (90 cents) plus a deposit of 15 pf per bottle. There are 100 pf in a DM and the notation used for 1.5 DM is 1,5 DM. 95% of all bottles are returnable half litres that come in two shapes. Most stores will take any returnable. Some small stores will take only returnables from the breweries they do business with, but this is lack of understanding on the part of the clerks. There is also a deposit of 3-4 DM on the plastic cases and these are only returnable at a store that deals in the beer named on the case. In a *getränkemarkt* (beverage store) or in a grocery store with a *getränke* section, there may be 2-3 dozen brands, about half of which will be local and the others from nearby cities. Prices generally range from 80 pf (50 cents) to 1,70 DM ($1.10) plus deposit. In a gas station, you may find 2-3 local brews and as many as a dozen big name brews from cities like Munich, Nurnberg and Frankfurt. There may even be beers from the other end of the country. Prices here will range from 2-3 DM ($1.20-1.80) plus deposit. Some gas stations have a getränkemarkt attached and their prices will be at beverage store level. A restaurant or gasthaus bar will also sell you beer by the bottle (for off premises consumption), but at the served price (about 3 DM). This may be the only way a given brand can be obtained. Beer can also be purchased directly from the brewery, but they will also usually charge you the served price because they all have a gasthaus or restaurant and that is how you access their brews. Several times I was able to buy beer from a brewery only because I had empty bottles to exchange for the full ones. The Germans are very conscious of costs. After hours, or on holidays when the establishment is closed, the beer may be more expensive, but they are obtainable. I have bought beer from chambermaids and charwomen after closing time.

So, on a religious holiday, with everything closed except gas stations, we scavenged for brews throughout Schwäbia and the Schwarzwald, a more or less rectangular path from Stuttgart to Villingen-Schwenningen to Offenburg to Karlsruhe to Stuttgart. It took a bit more effort than usual (and certainly a lot of gas stations), but there were significant results. The following reports are of beers found this day and sampled over the next few days (as we found too many to taste in a single day).

As you head south from Stuttgart, the first major towns you meet are Tübingen and Reutlingen. The local beers of the area (made in nearby Bad Urach and Metzingen) were found as follows: **Klosterbrauerei Gmbh.** (Metzingen Bräustätte Stuttgart, a subsidiary of Robert Leicht) in Metzingen produces **BRÄUCHLE HELLER BOCK** — pale golden amber, attractive lightly toasted malt aroma, big malt flavor, nicely carbonated and this balances the malt more than hops, big body, very long aftertaste; **SIGEL KLOSTER KRISTALL-WEIZEN** — brilliant gold, big head, sweet nose with a clove background, also seemed to be a faint sense of acetone, flavor is somewhat candy-like with the lactic acid (cloves) in competition rather than balanced, finish is a bit sweet with citrus in behind, fairly short aftertaste has some banana; **SIGEL KLOSTER HEFE-WEIZEN** — hazy amber, big head, dry malt aroma, dry malt flavor shows some cloves as well, fair to good body, complex, medium long dry aftertaste of malt and faint cloves; **SIGEL KLOSTER PILSENER** — a dull and uninteresting pils; and **SIGEL KLOSTER HEFE-WEISSBIER** — gold, big hop nose, malt flavor, a bit dull, light dry malt aftertaste with medium length. All have been seen only in their local marketing area.

From **Privatbrauerei Karl Olpp** of Bad Urach, we tasted **URACHER OLPP HELL** — bright gold, hop and grain nose and taste, very drinkable and refreshing, medium body, short duration, not done in a German style; **BAD URACH OLPP DOPPELBOCK** — copper-brown, sweet malt nose, big malt and hop flavor, balanced, delicious, smooth, long malt and hop aftertaste, very likeable and the 8.1% alcohol is not at all obtrusive; and **BAD URACH OLPP MAIBOCK** — brilliant gold, big rich dry malt aroma, excellent balance, great dry malt and hop flavor, unbelievably smooth, alcohol not really noticeable although 8.1%, just seems to smooth it off even more, long dry malt and hop aftertaste, a big winner. Please note that the word *bad* means bath, so that Bad — means the town is or was a health spa. Lunching at Schloss Lichtenstein we found **QUENZER SPEZIAL EXPORT** — tawny-gold, beautiful hop nose, smooth malt flavor with a mild hop finish, long dry hop aftertaste. This beer is from **Quenzer-Bräu Gmbh.** of Bad Urach and this was the only time we saw it despite a saturation search of area stores. By the way, Schloss Lichtenstein is worth a visit. The castle was built in the mid-1880s, replacing an earlier structure, but when they built it they drew upon a lot of imagination. They did a great job and it is the picture of a classical romantic fantasy perched on a high narrow peak with its walls becoming one with the cliff face.

The Tuttlingen area produces as many brews as many major German cities. There are breweries in Tuttlingen, Mohringen, Geislingen and Wurmlingen. Although we found many brands, I feel that we only scratched the surface here. **Kronenbrauerei Otto Kimer Söhne** in Tuttlingen/Möhringen offers **KRONEN PILS** — gold, hop nose with plenty of supporting malt, slightly sour hop flavor well-backed with malt, long dry sour hop aftertaste; **KRONEN GOLD EXPORT** — gold, light malt and hop nose, off-dry malt flavor, dry hop finish, long hop and malt aftertaste; **KRONEN BRÄU VOLLBIER** — gold, faint hop nose, fairly rich malt flavor, finishes dry hops like the Pils, long dry sour hop aftertaste; **KRONEN WEIZEN EXPORT** — gold, big head, fresh clove aroma, clean and bright spicy clove and malt flavor, balanced, refreshing, feels good in your mouth, long dry spicy aftertaste, an excellent and very drinkable weizen; and **KIRNER'S AECHT BADENER** — gold, nice hop nose, some complexity, rather ordinary malt palate, smooth and only lightly hopped, not much of an aftertaste. **Familienbrauerei Link** in Tuttlingen-Möhringen produces the very fine **MÖHRINGEN HERRENHAUS PILS**, a superbly balanced rich tasting brew loaded with both malt and hops, long and lusty, it is a super beer. In Wurmlingen, **Hirsch Brauerei Honer** makes a trio of brews: **HIRSCH HONER PILS** — light gold, pleasant hop nose, smooth lightly hopped flavor, light body, light dry hop aftertaste, light everything; **HIRSCH GOLD EXPORT** — pale gold, faint malt nose, pleasant light malt flavor, almost no hops at all, dry malt aftertaste has good length, but the brew simply needs more hop character; **JAEGERHOF PILS** — gold, hop nose, very little flavor on the front of the palate, not much anywhere, dry hop finish and aftertaste, very short. All three could stand to be bigger. In Geislingen, **Brauerei Götx** produces **DIE DUNKLE BARTELSTEINER WEISSE** — hazy amber, light clove nose, spicy clove flavor, very dry finish and it sort of dies at that point, leaving only some faint sourness as an aftertaste.

Soon after leaving Tuttlingen, we found ourselves in the central Schwarzwalder or Black Forest and in Fürstenberg territory. Remembering that Pabst used to import this really fine beer, we decided to try it in Donauschingen, home of the brewery. Made by **Fürstlich Fürstenbergische Brauerei, K.G.**, we tasted **FÜRSTENBERG PILS** for the first time in many years. I am glad to say that this bright golden beer still has the smooth malt and hop aroma, big nicely balanced hops, soft smooth light hop finish and aftertaste, good complexity and length, great mouth feel and a pleasure to drink.

Rottweil is famous for those big black and tan dogs and its photogenic setting, but is also famous for a dark beer **ORIGINAL ROTT-WEILER SCHWARZBIER** deep rosy-brown brew, with a pleasant dry lightly toasted malt nose, a burnt nature on the palate gives the malt more complexity, faint dry malt aftertaste, but dies immediately as it is swallowed leaving little after, also the balance is questionable. Another brewery in town is **Pflugbrauerei Rottweil.** Its beer is **SCHWARZ-WÄLDER URTYP-EXPORT**, a gold brew with a very faint malt nose, faint malt flavor and a brief malt aftertaste. Working our way further into the Schwarzwalder we found two pleasant but not remarkable beers from **Privatbrauerei Graf-Eder Gmbh. & Co., K.G.** The Graf Brewery in Oberndorf produces **OBERNDORFER PRIVAT** — gold, mild hop and malt nose, malt palate, light hops appear in the finish, dry wimpy hop aftertaste; and **OBERNDORFER PILSENER** — gold, big head, highly carbonated (you can even taste it), creamy, light malt and hop nose, dry malt flavor with a dry hop finish, medium long dry hop aftertaste.

In the center of the Schwarzwald in the attractive town of Alpirsbach is the Alpirsbacher Klosterbrauerei, one of the better known breweries in the region. They make **ALPIRSBACHER KLOSTER DUNKEL** — deep amber-brown, faint malt nose, medium body, very dry malt flavor, no complexity, light brief dry malt aftertaste; **ALPIRSBACHER KLOSTER HEFE WEIZEN** — hazy tawny-gold, off-dry wheaty malt aroma, off-dry wheat and barley malt flavor, no spicy tang, very long aftertaste like the flavor but a bit drier, fresh and clean in the mouth, very pleasant and refreshing; **ALPIRSBACHER KLOSTER KRI-STALLKLAR WEIZEN** — bright gold, faint slightly sweet malt aroma that is very clean, full body, rich malt flavor, well-balanced, refreshing, long off-dry fairly delicate aftertaste; **ALPIRSBACHER KLOSTER SPEZIAL** — bright tawny-gold, slightly sweet hop aroma, palate is off-dry malt up front, dry in the middle with a faint vegetal nature, finishes with both hops and malt leading into a long dry hop aftertaste with a faint sour vegetal malt background; and **ALPIRS-BACHER KLOSTER PILS** — bright tawny-gold, creamy head, faintly off-dry malt aroma with a hop backing, slightly sour malt front palate, very dry middle, sour malt and dry hop aftertaste. These brews have some popularity in Stuttgart and appear on many restaurant lists.

Leaving Villingen-Schwenningen took us through some very scenic Schwarzwald roads. The route from St. Georgen to Offenburg is especially beautiful driving in that direction. Some of the other roads going south off that route are also noted for their beauty.

The *Kaiserstuhl* or Emperor's Seat is a volcanic mass that is quite noticeable because it juts up from flat land. According to legend, Emperor Frederick Barbarossa lies on this mountain awaiting his second coming. The Barbarossa legend has played a part in German history as recently as fifty years ago when the founders of the Third Reich used references to it. From the Kaiserstuhl area near Freiburg comes another batch of brews. A pair of brews from the **Riegeler Brauerei** of Riegel/ Kaiserstuhl can easily catch your attention. **RIEGELER SPEZIAL EXPORT** is rated a mere excellent with its bright malt flavor, but the **RIEGELER FELSEN PILS** is outstanding with a spicy hop character from the Tettnanger hops which are grown locally. We did not have time to visit the city of Freiburg and found only one beer from there. It was **GANTER EXPORT** from **Privatbrauerei Ganter**, a typical export style with a big malty flavor, pleasant, but not remarkable.

Heading north along the western edge of the Schwarzwald, we travelled along parallel to the French border which is the Rhein River at that point passing the resort of Baden-Baden, a beautiful but touristy town that has been a spa since the Roman Imperial Baths were built there, nearing Karlsruhe before swinging off east to Stuttgart and our base camp. On the way we picked up the beers of the **Badische Staatsbrauerei** in Rothaus. **ROTHAUS DUNKEL EXPORT** was an excellent big and tasty roasted malt brew, not complex but simply a delight for lovers of roasted malt flavor. **ROTHAUS MÄRZEN** was an exceptionally smooth malty beverage. **ROTHAUS PILS** was bright, clean and malty. They all were good, but **ROTHAUS TANNEN ZAPFLE** took the prize. It was a big, smooth, dry hop and malt brew that is just luscious. It is also widely available and very popular. At Rastatt, there was **AUGUST HATZ PRIVAT** from **Hofbrauhaus Hatz**. This was a big bright beer with plenty of malt on the palate, a zesty hop aftertaste and an excellent balance throughout. Also found in Rastatt was **Brauerei Franz** and **TURKENLOUIS BOCKBIER** a pale amber brew with a rich malt nose, big rich malt flavor, big body, some hops but mostly malt, very satisfying and filling brew and a very long malt aftertaste. If you need to walk off some brews, Rastatt offers tours of the Neues Schloss and two interesting museums (the Wehrgeschichtliches Museum with its military memorabilia and the Freiheitsmuseum which traces the history of German liberalism—think about that for a moment). There are also tours of Schloss Favorite located between Baden-Baden and Rastatt.

Swinging past Karlsruhe we found **E. Winkels KG** and **WINKELS MEISTER BRÄU PILSENER** — gold, big hop nose that was extremely fragrant, you could smell it a good two feet away, lusty malt flavor well-balanced with hops, long bitter hop aftertaste, best described as a big rough and tumble brew; **WINKELS MEISTER BRÄU EXPORT** — gold, big malt and hop nose, finely carbonated, balanced malt and hop flavor, smooth and delicious, long bright hop aftertaste; and **WINKELS MEISTER BRÄU HEFE WEIZEN** — hazy gold, medium head, pleasant malt nose with a tartness in back, zesty malt and clove flavor, good balance set between the sweetness of the malt and the tartness of the lactic acid, complex and refreshing, long aftertaste follows the flavor in kind. We also found a single label (but a great find) from **Brauerei Moninger** of Karlsruhe. The great find was **MONINGER BERTHOLD BOCK DUNKEL** — brown, lovely rich and roasted dry malt nose, good carbonation level, rich dry malt flavor, hops join with the carbonation to balance the richness of the malt, long rich malt aftertaste, excellent brew. Should you have the opportunity to stay in town, Karlsruhe is noted for the quality of its museums.

The fourth day dawned bright and cloudless. Four consecutive days of beautiful weather in Germany is most fortunate, although most likely in May. From autumn to spring I have frequently referred to Germany as wet, cold and grey. From May through September is quite good with

hot and humid stretches being rare. Still, we were very pleased to hit an exceptionally nice period for our pilgrimage. This day we headed to the north and northeast of Stuttgart, toward Heilbronn, more noted for its wines than its beers. Heilbronn's big brewery is **Brauerei Cluss A.G.**, a most prolific brewery. First we found **CLUSS PILSENER,** a good tasting brew that was more malt than hops, but had plenty of both. Despite being overly carbonated, it was still quite good. **CLUSS RATSHOF PILS** was pleasant, light and dry. It was another good tasting brew, but not as big as the Cluss Pilsener. **CLUSS EXPORT** was well hopped behind the malt and good and smooth. **CLUSS KELLER PILS** was a big hoppy brew, but lacked balance. **CLUSS BOCK DUNKEL** had a big malt Ovaltine-like nose and had a very complex rich malt flavor but lighter than promised by the aroma. **DUTTENBERGER ENGELBRÄU URTYP** has a big flavor that is mostly malt, but definitely big.

Just west of Heilbronn is Eppingen and **Brauerei Palmbräu Zorn Sohne** offering **PALMBRÄU PILSENER**, a good hoppy brew with plenty of malt for balance and a long long dry hop aftertaste and **PALMBRÄU KRAICHGAU EXPORT**, a beer that was just too faint and too short to be of interest. The Palmbräu beers were also seen in the Heidelberg area,

Heading east out of Heilbronn, we drove through pleasant countryside that was largely rolling hills of farmland dotted with patches of light forest. This area is known as the Schwäbisch-Fränkischer Wald. We were headed toward the picturesque town of Rothenburg, a definite must for tourists. On the way is a small brewery **Privatbrauerei Gebr. Krauss** in Riedbach. Their **FRANKEN BRÄU PILS** is a bright hoppy beer and **FRANKEN BRÄU SPEZIAL**, a malty beer with a spicy hop background. Neither of these wander far from home. They are pleasant, but nothing special.

Rothenburg is an old feudal village that has been well preserved (it hasn't been of any military significance in hundreds of years) and has turned into a tourist town. It is the most famous medieval village in Germany, but is totally tourist oriented. It is very beautiful, worth a visit for sure, worth taking many photographs, but is concentrated tourism. One guide book recommended staying there as the only way to see the town without the tourists, early in the morning before they come or late evening after they have left. There are shops that sell just about everything that a tourist could want, but we did not find any new beers. We did find what we wanted in the nearby village of Reichelshofen, the site of **Privatbrauerei Fam. Wörner** and the Landwehr-Bräu Hotel. This is a spot worthy of note on any beer tour: an excellent restaurant, a beautiful hotel with 30 rooms and some marvelous beer. **ROTHENBURGER LANDWEHR PILSENER** was a big full-flavored long lasting mouthful with an abundance of hops and malt and about as good as any pilsener is going to be. **ALT FRANKISCH DUNKEL** was even better, a huge malty brew that was extremely smooth despite its heft, richly flavored and dry at the end. It was very good in bottle and super on draft. **ROTHENBURGER EXPORT EDELHELL** was a pleasant brew with good malt and a slightly sour hop flavor. Only the **ROTHENBURGER SCHANKBIER**, a low-alcohol beer at 2.2%/vol, failed to impress.

Landwehr-Bräu Hotel in Reichelshofen, near Rothenburg.

This would be an excellent place to dine and to lodge, but even though we were there well out of season, the dining room and hotel were fully booked on that day. Reservations would be in order as this facility is very near to Rothenburg and its large tourist draw.

Wandering a bit further to the east, we came to Wassertrüdlingen and the **Brauerei zum Schwarze Adler** and **PRIVAT WEIZEN HEFE-WEIZEN**, which was pleasantly spicy, but too lightly flavored. **Brauhaus Oettinger** in nearby Oettinger, did better with a very tasty **OETTINGER DUNKLES HEFEWEIZEN** that was more like a draft beer than any weizen we had tasted in a bottle. A big amber-brown beer with a huge thick head, the aroma was light and spicy, but the flavor was robust and long. **OETTINGER HEFEWEISSBIER**, the paler version of the above, was pleasant and spicy, but lacked the zest of its brown brother. **OETTINGER PILS** was strong and long hops and **OETTINGER EXPORT** was beautifully balanced with plenty of hops and malt. The Oettinger beers are worth seeking.

Still with plenty of sunshine left, we reached out a bit further to Treuchtlingen, which appeared big enough to offer us some new tastes. In this town is an old friend, **Privatbrauerei Rudolf Schäff/Schäffbräu. SCHÄFF FEUREFEST EDEL BIER** graced American store shelves for several years and if you didn't try it (as it was very expensive, like $5 per bottle), you missed one of the world's most interesting beers. We remembered it as a big smoky-roasted malt sipping beer with little or no carbonation, more like a malt liqueur. I had a ten year old bottle once and it was unchanged by age. Today we were looking for Schäff's other brews and found **ALTMÜHLTALER PILSENER** — pale gold, big hop nose, hefty body, strong hop and malt flavor, dry hop aftertaste has a sourness that causes it to end poorly; **ALTMÜHLTALER SCHLOSSBRAUEREI URTYP HELL** — gold, big strong hop nose, dull hop flavor, off-dry soft dry hop aftertaste; and **SCHÄFF PILSENER** — pale gold, light hop aroma, highly carbonated, palate starts off as strong hops, softens toward middle where some malt joins in to set the balance, malt finish, long slightly sour malt and hop aftertaste.

Heading back, we entered Ellwangen as our good weather began to turn. After parking the car, a light rain began to fall as we walked to the **Gasthaus Brauerei Roter Ochsen.** The cheery red facade of the building matched the warmth of the interior and the zest of the beers. This is another great place to stay on a beer pilgrimage. There is a large guest house with 40 rooms, a fine restaurant with a large menu and some excellent beers. Run by the Veit family and also known as Brauerei Hermann Veit, the brewery offers six fine beers on a regular basis. **ELLWANGER ROTOCHSEN TRADITIONSBOCK** at 6.6% alc/vol was a rich, creamy, toasted malt brew, a big long dry lip smacking beer that is one of the top ten finds of our search. **STIFTSHERREN PILS** was dry and hoppy and very long while the **EDEL EXPORT** was smooth and malty with the hops bouncing out from behind and holding the balance. I have to recommend the **ELLWANGER ROTOCHSEN DUNKLES HEFE-WEIZEN** as a big bodied, complex, long, spicy brew that is excellent of type. The **ELLWANGER ROTOCHSEN KRISTALL-WEIZEN** was pleasantly malted with a faint clove background and the **ELLWANGER HEFE-WEIZEN**, with its robust clove and malt flavor would perform at the top of most tastings except they were dwarfed by the Bock and the dark Hefe-weizen. This establishment is highly recommended except that it is difficult to park near.

On the rest of the day's journey, we drove through showers of rain. Few new brews made their appearance. **MEISTERBRÄU EXPORT** from **Brauerei Ladenburger** of Neuler was too sweet and brief to be of interest. **Brauerei Lang** of Schwäbisch Gmünd has a beer of interest mostly because it is in a metal can with a snap top. It is **LA BIERE DE LA GRANDE ARMÉE** which has a luscious malt aroma with some toasted quality and dry smoked sausage, creamy texture with small bubble carbonation, rich toasted malt flavor and a long aftertaste like the flavor, but attenuated. More familiar to Americans is the Engel Brauerei of Schwäbisch Gmund since we have seen **TYROLIAN BRÄU BEER**, **ST. BERNARD BRÄU BEER** and the excellent **ANGEL BREW BEER** in our stores. We found two new ones, both with interesting names: **TROMPE LA MORT DOUBLEBOCK** — deep gold with an amber tinge, rich malt aroma, very rich malt flavor, big body, huge, very strong and very long dry malt aftertaste and **BIERE DES DRUIDES** (With a name like that, how can one resist?) — hazy yellow, toasted malt nose and flavor, malt finish and aftertaste, good while it is in your mouth, but it quits as soon as you swallow it.

On To Bavaria: The Beer Pilgrim's Paradise

The next day dawned more typical of the area, spotty sunshine through grey clouds with occasional sprinkles. We decided to put in some miles before resuming the hunt, just to get out of turf we had well beaten during the past few days. The next big city on the autobahn was Ulm, famous for the Münster, its great cathedral with the highest church spire in the world. The 160 meter spire of the west wall is visible for a considerable distance as you approach Ulm. Construction of the Münster was begun in the 14th century and there was great difficulty in creating that very tall spire, so great that it was not fully completed until the late 19th century. Even yet, there are problems. Thirty years ago, when I first saw the structure, it was surrounded by scaffolding and being repaired. I have seen it without the scaffolding infrequently, and it was being worked on again in 1991. On that Saturday morning, we found that the huge square before the church is the site of a farmers' market. There was absolutely no place to park. After about a half hour, we quit the circling throng, just missing a space now and then, and looked for some beer on the outskirts. We wanted to visit the church, but could not this Saturday morning. Besides, the repair work had much of the access closed off.

The local beers we found were some from **Ulmer Münster Brauerei**. They were **MÜNSTER WEIHNACHTS BIER** — deep gold, rich toasted malt aroma, full rich malt flavor, very complex and smooth, finely balanced, creamy, fairly long dry malt aftertaste; **ULMER MÜNSTER ZUNFTMEISTER SPEZIAL DUNKEL** — medium pale amber, nice toasted malt nose, palate has a big malt front, smooth middle making the transition to a hop finish, delicious, long complex dry

23

hop and malt aftertaste, good body, good beer; **ULMER MÜNSTER KANZLERGOLD HELLES STARKBIER** — faintly hazy amber-gold, complex malt nose with chocolate, Ovaltine and Postum -like features, equally complex malt flavor, pleasant and very long malt aftertaste; **RATS KRONE HELL** — gold, good malt-hop nose, smooth malt flavor with the hops in back, good dry malt finish, long dry malt and hop aftertaste; **RATS KRONE PILS** — gold, beautiful hop nose, good flavor with plenty of both malt and hops, long dry malt and hop aftertaste, good tasting beer; **LÖWENBRÄU NEU-ULM WEIZEN** — gold, bright big spicy nose, creamy, big sparkle on the tongue, clean flavor feels good and is refreshing, plenty of spice and zest, long bright spicy aftertaste, a delightful beer; **WAPPEN PILS** — gold, big malt nose and flavor, hardly any hops except in the aftertaste, pleasant but not exciting, brief aftertaste; and **HIRSCH BIER URHELL** — medium deep gold, vegetal-malt nose, malt flavor, dry malt finish and aftertaste, not much offered.

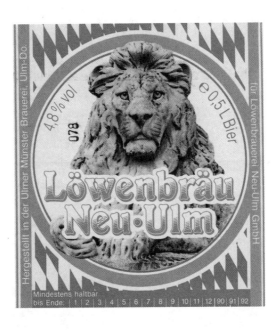

There is another brewery in Ulm, **Gold Ochsen, Gmbh.,** but we found only familiar ones that once had been exported to the U.S. They are worthy beers to try, however, and I can remember some marvelous venison and other wild game dinners made even more memorable with Gold Ochsen. Thinking of food for the moment, German restaurants offer the best milk-fed veal I have ever had, excellent pork and a variety of game dishes. Venison, wild boar, pheasant and trout frequently pop up on menus. Also a wide variety of sauces are offered for your *schnitzel* (cutlet) or you may just want to eat the greatest wiener schnitzel imaginable. A couple of my favorite styles are *Jäeger* (hunter style-a heavy rich brown sauce loaded with mushrooms) and *Zigeuner* (gypsy style-a spicy rich brown sauce with peppers). The German restaurants occasionally offer unusual dishes like shank, which take a long time to prepare. *Schweinehaxen* or *Lammhaxen* (pork or lamb shank) are worth looking for as blackboard specials. Sauerbraten is rarely seen. Beef and chicken are expensive in Germany and not seen as often although they are available more now than they used to be. For beef try a *rumpsteak* or something like beef *Rouladen*, rolled thin steak filled with mushrooms, onions, etc. Balanced meals with salad and lots of vegetables are usually offered and attractively presented. If you are bold enough, you may try *Blutwurst* (blood sausage), the country head cheese and patés and some of the other local specialties. Always bring your dictionary and don't be afraid to ask. I always laugh when I think of the man who ordered kidneys when he thought he was ordering onions. Of course I let him do it. The kidneys were good, too. In the spring watch for *Spargel*, the great white asparagus. Germans do not let asparagus grow like we do. Each morning they go out and mound earth on top of the shoots as they try to come out into the sunshine. The shoots keep trying and the Germans keep covering them. Eventually they harvest the result, a huge thick long white asparagus. Restaurants all over Germany offer these in May, either by themselves, as a side dish or in a soup. They are a bit pricey, but if you are in Germany in May, you must try them at least once.

That morning we found a few other brews to try from nearby towns. One of the more interesting was from **Brauerei Convikt** in Dillengen am Donau, **CONVIKT EGAUER ZWICK'L DUNKLES KELLER-BIER** — bright copper-amber, light roasted malt nose, faintly sweet and grainy malt flavor, quite pleasant, finely carbonated, good balance, medium body, finishes even better than it starts with a good long medium dry roasted malt aftertaste. Another was from **Radbrauerei Gebr. Bucher** of Günzburg; **GÜNZBURGER HEFE-WEIZEN** — hazy gold, faint spicy nose, good well-spiced clove and malt flavor, high carbonation, flavor is on the light side and the carbonation interferes, smooth, light to medium body, light brief spicy aftertaste. There were a trio from **Brauerei Schwarzbräu**, a brewery in Zusmarshausen: **SCHWARZBRÄU PILSENER** — gold, hop nose, big hop flavor, good body and balance, very long good dry hop aftertaste; **SCHWARZBRÄU EXQUISIT SPEZIALBIER** — gold, malt and hop nose, big malt flavor with a hop finish, dry hop aftertaste is very dry and very long, huge body, a big mouthful of flavor; and **SCHWARZBRÄU DUNKLES EXPORT WEIZEN** — hazy brown, head like a *fass* (draft) beer, clean spicy nose, very pleasant fruity-spicy flavor, nicely balanced, good body and a long dry malt aftertaste. Last, we found a pair from **Postbrauerei Thannhausen**, a brewery in Thannhausen: **POSTBRÄU BERNHARDI GOLD SPEZIAL MÄRZEN** — gold, big hop aroma, malt flavor has plenty of hop support, big body, richness goes all the way through the palate into the aftertaste, long rich malt aftertaste goes dry at the end; and **POSTBRÄU HEFE-WEIZEN** — hazy gold, odd dull malt aroma, pleasant bright and clean spicy clove and malt palate, medium body, short dry malt aftertaste.

We knew of another Brauereigasthof just south of Ulm and decided to try their beers with lunch. It was getting colder and rainy and we needed the warmth of a hot kitchen and some good beer. **Privatbrauerei Gasthof Schmid/Brauerei Biberach** was a bit difficult to find. We knew it to be in Biberach, but only Roggenburg shows on most maps, if that does. It is on the road from Weissenhorn to Krumbach and the Johann Schmid's establishment is about half of the town. There is no hotel, but there is homemade bread, country paté, wurst and some very nice beer. This establishment matches the definition of a brew-pub, one that has been around since 1844, run by the same family. **BIBERACHER UR-DUNKEL** is dark brown, has a lovely malt nose, light body, smooth malt flavor and a pleasant dry malt aftertaste. **BIBERACHER MÄRZEN** is deep gold, has a hop nose with a faint yeasty-bready nature (but pleasantly so), good malt and hop flavor, good balance, rich taste, good body, dry malt-hop finish and aftertaste and is very good with German country wursts and patés. The former was our impression on draft at the gasthof and the following is how it was a few days later in the bottle: **BIBERACHER MÄRZEN** — amber, light malt aroma and flavor, very little hops, low carbonation, pleasant and smooth, light short malt aftertaste. Actually, I find it interesting that they should be that different. Probably a different batch.

Brauerei Gasthof Schmid in Roggenburg.

It was at this gasthof that we first encountered the beers of **Schlossbrauerei Autenried** as Schmid had their weizen to satisfy demand for a beer he did not wish to brew. I still cannot find Autenreid on the map, but I did find a number of their brews in the area south of Ulm and I include them here: **AUTENRIEDER WEIZEN** — hazy gold, big thick head, clean malt aroma, smooth malt flavor, very refreshing, faint trace of cloves is way in back of nose and palate, good body, good balance, long dry malt aftertaste; **AUTENRIEDER PILSNER** — gold, fragrant hop nose, good hop flavor, long dry hop aftertaste has a bit of sourness at the end; **AUTENRIEDER URTYP HELL** — deep gold, light malt aroma, malt flavor, hops in back, dry malt aftertaste; and **AUTENRIEDER URTYP DUNKEL** — brown, off vegetal (garbage) nose, taste to match the bad aroma, dull dry malt aftertaste.

The gasthof was ready to close up as soon as the lunch period was over as there was some local celebration that everyone was going to attend, so we took off cross country toward Augsburg to rejoin the autobahn to Munich.

Near Geltendorf, south of Augsburg and west of Munich is found the famous **Sclossbrauerei Kaltenberg** (Irmingard Prinzessin von Bayern Gmbh.), the brewery at Schloss Kaltenberg, with the Prinz Regent as the royal brewmaster. The castle is classical Bavarian in style and has structures dating to the 13th century, although most of it has been built in the last two centuries. The beers are frequently found in remote parts of the country. The labels include **KÖNIG LUDWIG DUNKEL** — deep red-brown, light off-dry malt nose, smoky malt flavor, smokiness becomes overdone in the aftertaste; **KALTENBERG HELL** — gold, malt nose, high carbonation, vegetal malt flavor with hops in back, medium body, brief dull malt aftertaste; **PRINZREGENT LUITPOLD KÖNIGSLICHES DUNKLES WEISSBIER**— very slightly hazy brown, pleasant spicy clove nose, well-spiced flavor, finishes malty with the cloves removing to a supporting position, fairly short malt and spice aftertaste; and **PRINZREGENT LUITPOLD HEFE-WEISSBIER** — hazy gold, faintly spicy malt nose, rich alcoholic malt flavor with the spiciness taking a back seat, long dry malt and clove aftertaste. They do make a beer worthy of royalty.

Other finds from the region south of Ulm were: **Bierbrauerei Ott** in Bad Schussenried makes the uninteresting **OTT URTYP, SCHUS-SENRIEDER PILSENER**, a pleasant well-hopped brew with a dry hop finish and aftertaste, and **OTT SPEZIAL**, an enjoyable balanced beer with a pleasant hop and malt nose and flavor, good body and long dry hop and malt aftertaste. There was also **BURGER & ENGELBRAU VOLLBIER HELL** from **Burger & Engelbrau A.G.** of Memmingen. This golden brew has a rich malt nose, beautifully balanced smooth flavor with more malt than hops, is quite dry and, though a bit light, is fairly long and very drinkable.

Augsburg is one of the oldest cities in Germany, but little of it survived 1944 as it was the location of the Messerschmidt airplane factory. In the city we found **Hasen-Brau A.G.**, a brewery with many labels. We tried **HASEN-BRÄU AUGSBURGER EXPORT** — bright gold, malt aroma and flavor, well-balanced and smooth, medium long dry malt aftertaste, pleasant but not exciting; **HASEN-BRÄU DOPPELBOCK DUNKEL** — brown, rich earthy malt aroma, rich full-flavored malt palate, very satisfying, sense of high alcohol, long rich malt aftertaste, real sipping beer; **HASEN-BRÄU EXTRA** — gold, hop nose, faint dull off-dry malt and hop flavor, medium body, even fainter aftertaste like the flavor; **HASEN-BRÄU HELL** — gold, light soapy hop nose, good malt and hop flavor, balanced, dry hop aftertaste with the malt laid back in behind; **BUNST BIER VOLLBIER HELL** — gold, slightly soapy hop nose, soapy flavor, hop finish, medium length slightly dry hop aftertaste; and **HASEN-BRÄU AUGSBURGER MÄRZEN** — gold, zesty hop and malt nose, big balanced malt and hop flavor, perky and alcoholic (5.7%), richly malted, long dry hop aftertaste, more like a heller bock than a Märzen. There was also **BAYRISCH HELL**

VOLLBIER from Augusta-Bräu. It was a deep golden brew with a light aroma that is mostly hops with faint malt in back, light malt and hop flavor, medium body and a medium to short light dry malt and hop aftertaste.

We swung around Munich on the ring road and down the autobahn toward Garmisch. We were tempted by the allure of this very famous beer city, but Munich is a big city and it was late in the day. It could keep until another day when we could do it justice. About 30 miles down the road, as we left the autobahn to travel eastward to Bad Tölz, I was also well aware that a few miles to the west was Andechs-Erling, home of my favorite beer. Monday, I thought to myself, remembering that big crowds go to the monastery on Sundays and it is hard to find a seat in the *Bierstube* or *Bierhalle* even on the coldest day of winter. Meanwhile, a warm fire, a big hot meal, some good beer and a warm bed were waiting for me in a little gasthaus on Tölzer Str. 4 in Reichersbeuren called the *Zum Altwirt*, (the old innkeeper). At least, we hoped there was, for the Altwirt has only about five rooms and we had no reservations. Since I am fond of using modestly priced digs, I rarely have a reservation in advance. Out of season, one rarely has difficulty. There are exceptions, like when the international book fair is going on in Frankfurt and you may have to go past Darmstadt to get a room, but outside of the big cities there always seems to be a gasthaus with an available room at a reasonable price. Zum Altwirt had a room for us (in fact, we were the only guests there) and we stayed there five nights as it is a great spot for a base camp at 70 DM (under $40) for a double.

Supper at the Altwirt is a treat of home cooking with big portions. Their *Altwirtsplatte* includes pork, beef, wild hare, potato croquettes, mushrooms in cream sauce and an ample garnish of vegetables, costing about 44 DM (approx $25) for two people. They also feature the beers from Maisach, a town just west of Munich. **Brauerei Maisach** offers a trio of excellent brews. **MAISACH RÄUBER-KNEISSL** is copper-brown, has a dry malt aroma and palate that, despite being dry is quite rich, has a big body and a long dry malt aftertaste. It is very satisfying and great with food. **MAISACH HELLER BOCK** is my favorite. This deep tawny-gold brew has a beautiful complex malt and hop aroma, so good it sends a shiver down your spine. It has a big body, delicious long

29

complex flavor of balanced hops and malt and a wonderful long after-taste that is a continuation of the flavor gradually becoming drier as it goes. This is about as good as a pale lager can get. **MAISACH BRAUEREI PILS** is bright gold, has a well-hopped aroma and a beautiful hop flavor, long dry hop aftertaste, good body and an excellent balance. It is a good example of a classic pils. Now, do you see why I like to stay at Zum Altwirt?

There is the **Grüner Bräu** brewery in Bad Tolz that makes four beers that I have found to be moderately interesting. **GRÜNER BIER DUNKEL** is dark brown, has a light malt aroma and taste, very little hop character, medium body and a short malt aftertaste. **GRÜNER EXPORT** is deep gold, has a light malt aroma and flavor, medium body, and has a medium long malt aftertaste. It is smooth and very drinkable. **TÖLZER EDEL WEIZEN** is hazy brown, has a light slightly lactic nose and flavor, medium body and a medium length malt aftertaste with a trace of the lactic spice which is more pronounced at the end. This hefeweizen is smooth and drinkable. **TÖLZER WEISSE** is bright gold, has a very light smooth malt nose and taste with only a trace of lactic-weizen character. It is very mild with a medium body and a mild malt aftertaste that has medium length and little spiciness. It is smooth and pleasant enough, but a bit weak for those who like their weizen to have zest.

Bad Tölz itself is a well-known spa, frequented for the most part by the elderly, although it frequently is used by German firms for sales conferences. It is a quiet town with many good restaurants and an interesting mainstreet from which vehicular traffic has been excluded. There is a *Metzgerei* (butcher shop) on the street from which come the most appetizing aromas as they cook up their sausages for the lunchtime crowd. The location of the town is simply beautiful, with the Isar river flowing at the foot of the Bavarian Alps.

The next day was Sunday and a somewhat cold and rainy one. Here in the Bavarian Alps, it can snow as easily as rain, almost any time of the year except July. Even though this was May, it was one of those grey, cold, wet days. Since we had no wish to traipse through a cold, grey, wet Munich, we headed east to that little corner of Germany near Austria so loved by Der Fuhrer. We could have lunch in Salzburg, Austria (including some deliciously obscene dessert) and walk out to the Königsee, one of the most beautiful and serene places on earth. Who knows, we might even find some brews.

Stopping to gas up just outside of town, we found that we were near **Weissbierbrauerei Hans Hopf** in Miesbach. They make **HOPF WEISSE EXPORT**, a *kristallklar* (crystal clear, yeast filtered out) with a light spicy malt aroma (not the usual cloves) that had a fruity background like apple and banana, a sweet malt and faint lactic acid palate that was a bit too sweet and did not have enough balancing factors to mitigate the sweetness, good body and a long, too sweet, malt aftertaste. Their other brew is **HOPF DUNKLE SPEZIAL DUNKLES HEFEWEISSBIER**, a clear deep amber-brown with a big head, hefty malt aroma, strong malt flavor (but no follow-thru) and a weak off-dry malt aftertaste. There were also some of the beers from Tegernsee, which we salted away for later, expecting to visit their great beer hall later in the afternoon on our return.

We caught up with the Munich-Salzburg autobahn near the Chiemsee, Bavaria's largest lake. This is a great tourist attraction. From the town of Prien you can catch a ferry to a number of islands. On Herrinsel Island is the Schloss Herrenchiemsee, one of the castles built by Ludwig II (Mad Ludwig), king of Bavaria in the late 19th century. It is a miniature of Versaille, reflecting Ludwig's adoration of the Sun King (Louis XIV) of France. The ferry/cruise boat takes you to the island and there you can spend a pleasant day among the beautiful gardens, fields and woods surrounding the castle. It is a lovely trip and a delightful place to wander about.

We motored in light rain straight through to Austria without stopping. At borders in the European Economic Community autos are simply waved through. No one seems to want to see a passport (quite a difference from past years). Salzburg was waiting for us with all kinds of tortes. It was chilly and drizzling in Salzburg (which it always seems to be when I am there), so we turned our thoughts to our palates. We did away with some delightful lunch including a couple of tortes in honor of Mozart and had a couple of Austrian beers for him too.

Our tummies full with goodies, we drove back into Germany and headed straight for the Königssee. There is a 2+ kilometer walk, mostly up hill, to this beauty spot, a placid lake surrounded by mountains that plunge sharply down into the depths. A boat ride and cable car is also available if you have time. We reached the scenic spot, stood there in awe of the beauty of it for many minutes, then silently walked back to the car park. From the boat dock to the car park is now the site of many shops and restaurants. We stopped to reward ourselves for the exercise and tasted the beers of **Hofbrauhaus Berchtesgaden**, the brewery in Berchesgaden. They were both quite pleasant and we felt properly rewarded. **BERCHTESGADENER BIER** was bright gold, had a pleasant malt and hop nose, big flavorful dry malt and hop taste, good body and balance and a long dry hop and malt aftertaste. **BERCHTESGADENER WEIZEN** was hazy gold, had a nice clean spicy-fruity malt nose, tangy zesty clove and malt palate and a long clean satisfying aftertaste like the flavor. It feels good in your mouth, very tasty and refreshing.

Hitler's famous summer home, sits on its perch atop a mountain peak called the Kehlstein, and is visible from the Königsee car park. The sun was breaking through the clouds now and the building shone brightly in the sky even though we were still in shadow. It reminded me of the feudal castles that overlooked the villages below and the villagers over whose lives the feudal lords held absolute power. Hitler was just a few centuries late. There is a bus that travels the precarious road up the mountain to the building that now houses a restaurant called the Eagle's Nest. For almost twenty years now there is no evidence whatever that Hitler ever even visited the place. Thirty years ago there were photographs of Hitler, Eva Braun and his military and political hierarchy placed on the walls of the rooms so you could see them as they were in the rooms where they had been. Thirty years ago you could drive the road yourself to its end at the massive copper colored doors of an elevator that took you the final 375 feet to the house. The elevator was decorated with the Nazi bevo eagle with its wings spread out over the swatstika below. That, and virtually all physical evidence of the Third Reich, vanished between 20-25 years ago. Nazi regalia is scarce in Germany and in the *trödelmarkts* (junk markets) and *flohmarkts* (flea markets) sells for a much higher price than it does in the U.S.

Working our way back to the autobahn, we stopped at a gas station and found some of the beers from nearby Traunstein. **Hofbrauhaus Traunstein** produces **HOFBRAUHAUS TRAUNSTEIN FÜRSTEN QUELL**, which has a dull malt flavor, dry malt and hop finish and aftertaste and is uninteresting. The **HOFBRAUHAUS TRAUNSTEIN ALBAIRISCH DUNKEL** — has a pleasant toasted malt aroma and creamy roasted malt flavor. Unfortunately, it has a dull dry malt finish and aftertaste; **HOFBRAUHAUS TRAUNSTEIN ALTBAIRISCH UR-WEIZEN** is deep amber-brown, has a faint malt nose, but a big spicy malt flavor and medium long malt aftertaste with a clove background. It is pleasant but lacks depth and strength; **HOFBRAUHAUS TRAUNSTEIN HOFBRÄU WEISSE** is cloudy gold, has a clean faintly spicy malt nose, big clove and malt flavor, lemony finish, good body, fine balance, a very complex and delicious, long fresh cinnamon and clove aftertaste and is a very interesting and very good sipping beer. Just when we were about to give up on them they came through with a winner. Hofbrauhaus Traunstein also uses the corporate name **Tochterfirma Weissbräu Gmbh**, making weissbier for Franz Inselkammer in Aying. Another Traunstein brewery is **Brauerei Kiesel**, whose products have been extensively distributed in the United States by Fred Huber and we saw nothing that was not already familiar to us back home.

The trip back was long enough to generate a thirst and we slaked it at **Herzoglich Bayerisches Brauhaus Tegernsee**. Located on the southeast shore of the beautiful lake called the Tegernsee, this lovely resort town reminds me much of some Cape Cod resorts as they were in the 1940s. Relaxed and pleasant, it is a place to gather one's resources for the fight of civilized living. No wonder people go here for "the Cure." There is a *Bräustüberl* in the north end of the Kloster made up of many rooms interconnecting for the length of the building. We found a table about three-quarters of the way down and joined some lovely people from Dachau for some serious stein lifting and toasting. It is a fun place and a stranger doesn't stay a stranger for very long. We started with **TEGERNSEE HELLER BOCK**, a bright golden beer with a hop aroma, big hop and malt flavor that is balanced and rich and a complex malt and hop finish that leads into a long dry malt aftertaste. Next we tried **QUIRINUS DUNKELER DOPPEL-BOCK**, a big brown beer with a lightly toasted malt nose and flavor, a bit on the sweet side but very complex and earthy with a dry malt finish, off-dry malt aftertaste, big body and excellent balance. It is absolutely delicious and very drinkable. Later that night, we tasted in bottle **TEGERNSEE DUNKEL EXPORT** — dark amber-brown, pleasant malt aroma, lovely roasted malt flavor, refreshing and drinkable, good body, good balance, very satisfying, medium long dry malt aftertaste; **BRAUHAUS TEGERNSEE DUNKLER DOPPELBOCK** — deep amber-brown, malt aroma and flavor, palate is sweet in front, off-dry in the middle and stays off-dry thereafter, good body, very good of the type, long off-dry malt aftertaste, quite enjoyable, but not one of the blockbusters; **TEGERNSEE SPEZIAL** — gold, hop aroma, excellent balanced hop and malt flavor, long dry hop aftertaste, good body and about as good a balance as you can imagine (this is the best in a German export style that I have tasted); and **TEGERNSEER HELL** — gold, lovely hop aroma, good hop and malt flavor, excellent balance, good body, long dry hop and malt aftertaste, a really good beer superbly balanced.

We had not eaten at the Brauhaus (except for some big white radishes our friends insisted we try) because our Michelin Guide told us that the next town, only about 5 km distant, had sensational restaurants. Rottach-Egern has become a favorite resort for older and more affluent Germans and did not disappoint us. We had a great meal that night and the next two nights as well as we tried three of those highly rated restaurants. Man does not live by beer alone. One notable one was the Gasthof Angermeier, about 3 km out of town in the direction of Sutteu. Their *hausgemachte gulasch* was excellent as was the venison with mushrooms, *preissel-beeren* (cranberries) and homemade *spätzle* (a doughy noodle very popular in southern Germany).

The next day was Monday and the brilliant sunshine woke us. The tops of the Alps were still shrouded in clouds, but it was a beautiful sunny day — perfect for a trip to the monastery at Andechs. **Kloster-brauerei Andechs** is a Kloster Brewery in Erling-Andechs dating back to the 15th century. Like most ancient structures in Germany, it sits atop a large knoll and can be seen for many miles as you approach. It presents one of those illusions that make it appear larger the further away you are from it. Over the years I have tasted several of their brews. There is **ANDECHS SPEZIAL HELL**, a pale gold brew with a complex off-dry malt and hop aroma, bright complex zesty very malty flavor, full body, rich clean malt finish

Kloster Andechs.

and a fairly long aftertaste. There is also **ANDECHS EXPORT DUNKEL**, a deep amber-brown beer with a lovely toasted malt nose, good dry toasted malt flavor that is complex with lots of other underlying flavors like fruit, spices, aromatics, etc., has a medium body, dry malt finish and a long lightly burnt malt aftertaste. One of their bigger and more alcoholic brews is **ANDECHS BERGBOCK HELL**, a brilliant deep golden beer with a lovely nose that is mostly hops but is well-backed with malt, a big malt and hop flavor that is really smooth. It is a creamy, vinous beer with a very long malt aftertaste. The other beers may be good, but to me there is only one beer to have at Andechs — the **ANDECHS DOPPELBOCK DUNKEL**. Deep amber-brown, this double bock has an extremely rich malt nose that is very complex and has all kinds of earthy notes, a very complex flavor that seems to flip back and forth from dry to off-dry, again with all kinds of flavors weaving in and out. Some say it has an earthy quality, but I like the word funky. I told this to Hubie Smith (beer writer and brewmaster at Pizza Deli in Seattle) one time when he was on his way to Germany, and he told me that he couldn't imagine what that was like. When he returned he called to tell me that funky was the perfect description, but he still couldn't tell me what it meant. It also has a very long dry malt aftertaste. I believe this to be my favorite beer in all the world.

The rococo interior of the church is beautiful to the eye, and the quiet courtyards and passageways provide the required monastic atmosphere. The old original brewing equipment is on display behind glass while the modern brewing plant hides behind the knoll far below the religious buildings. The beer halle and stube awaited us. On a late Monday morning, most of the patrons were men of the town, who had climbed the hill carrying their lunch to enjoy everybody's favorite beer. I saw only the dark double bock being served. Food is served there and we acquired some wursts and breads to help us with our beer and, like the dozens of others around us, whiled away a pleasant hour or two.

Walking down the hill to the *Parkplatz* at Klosterbrauerei Andechs, we were experiencing more than just a little buzz from the alcohol. It runs about 6.5%, a good 30% more than your average German beer. A beer pilgrim in Germany must always be aware that the alcohol in these beers is higher than most of the brews he normally encounters. With many American beers, the alcohol is low enough that they can be consumed continuously over long stretches of time with little or no impairment of function, providing that they are not taken too rapidly. The same pace that would result in minimal impairment in the U.S. could cause considerable loss of reasoning ability and motor function in Germany. When soldiers are posted to U.S. military bases in Germany, part of the indoctrination is a warning about the strength of alcohol in the beer, and there are posters prominently displayed around the base. Some of the bocks reach 8%, the level of many of the local wines.

The beer tourist can't afford to become inebriated. First, it would cut into your drinking. Second, if you are driving a car, it makes it tough to find the next beer, especially if there are trees, pedestrians, walls and other cars in your path. Third, as you impair your functions, you interfere with your ability to judge the merit of a beer and it gets in the way of your enjoyment. It is simply bad form. Before we quit Erling-Andechs, we strolled through the town until our heads cleared. That we had allowed ourselves the luxury of a buzz was unusual and due simply to the high quality of the brew at this place and the potency of its alcohol. We always ate food with the beer. We always ordered only the smallest available size and then shared so as to minimize any effects of alcohol. If there were four beers on tap at a tavern, we bought one each of the four and each of us tasted them in turn. Many of the beers tasted were found packaged and we tasted those at night after dinner in our hotel, so we would not be driving after the tasting. Even then, we frequently went for a walk to clear the alcohol from the system after these night tastings. Alcohol doesn't have to be an enemy for most of us, but it is a factor that must be considered at all times.

We headed southward from Andechs toward the many great tourist attractions in the Garmisch-Partenkirchen area. In doing so we continued to run across beers from small brewers. There was **Dachsbräu**, a brewery in Weilheim with **DACHS WEIZEN**, a hazy brown brew with a pleasant spicy malt aroma and flavor and a long dry malt and spice aftertaste. Also in Weilheim there is the **Bräuwastl** brewery with **BRÄUWASTL KRISTALLWEIZEN** — slightly hazy amber, big head, complex malt aroma was relatively dry, barley malt and wheat about 50-50 on the palate, nice balance, very smooth, brief malt aftertaste, but a good tasting brew. There was also **Brauerei Karg** in Murnau am Staffelsee. Their two offerings were **KARG WEISSBIER** — hazy gold, fresh spicy nose and taste, creamy, finishes malt, spicy malt aftertaste, long, clean and refreshing; and **SCHWARZER WOIPER-LINGER DUNKLES HEFE-WEISSBIER** — cloudy brown, spicy nose, spicy malt flavor is smooth and creamy, fine balance, long dry spicy malt aftertaste, good body, excellent beer with rich foods and a marvelous beer just by itself.

We turned off the main road shortly before reaching Garmisch-P (as it is called on signs) and headed toward the very pretty town of Oberammergau, home of the world famous Passion Play, held every ten years (the next one is in 2000). Even when there is no event, the town is crowded with tourists looking to buy woodcarvings and other artifacts in the dozens of shops. There are also many fine restaurants and hotels. Every building is beautiful with its decorative paintings. There are also a couple of small grocery stores with a large assortment of beers, mostly from Munich.

Before you arrive at Oberammergau, you come to Ettal, site of a small health resort and a large Benedictine Kloster that makes a *Weinbrand* (wine brandy) and four beers, one of which is a double bock. The brewery is named **Klosterbrauerei Ettal Gmbh.** and offers **ETTALER KLOSTER DUNKEL** a deep tawny-amber brew with a light malt aroma, flavor of mostly malt except for a good hop finish, some complexity, good balance and a long dry malt and hop aftertaste. It is a very drinkable brew; **ETTALER CURATOR DUNKLER DOPPELBOCK**, a deep rosy-amber beer with a rich off-dry malt nose (almost sweet) and flavor, good body, high alcohol and a rich long slightly sour malt aftertaste; **ETTALER KLOSTER WEISSBIER**, a hazy gold wheat beer with a faint malt nose, delicate refreshing flavor of wheat, malt and cloves that is very good up front, softens a bit at the middle, but stays good and has a fairly long aftertaste like the flavor; **ETTALER KLOSTER WEISSBIER DUNKEL**, the dark version of the foregoing beer, which had a faint lightly spiced wheat beer nose, light clove and malt flavor, light body, spicy finish and a fairly long aftertaste like the flavor, but much lighter.

Other major tourist attractions in the immediate area is Linderhof Castle and the Wies Kirche. Linderhof was the summer home of Ludwig II and, although small, is a beautiful building outfitted with a collection of furniture and art. The grounds and gardens are a pleasure to walk. When you see the grotto, you will have to admit that, even though old Ludwig was considered mad, he had a lot of class. In the grotto is a golden conch in which Ludwig sat, dragged through the water with a mechanical arrangement, so he could enjoy Tannhaüser in the proper setting with his friend Wagner. It is worth a visit. The Wies Kirche is the world's best known example of rococo design. Even if you don't like cherubs, it is required viewing. It will knock your eyes out. It is important enough to be listed a World Heritage Site by UNESCO.

We decided on Füssen for lunch. I had lunched and dined there many times before and knew of several good restaurants which carried the local beer. Another advantage to lunching in Füssen was that there were two more castles there to afford the opportunity of working off that lunch. On our way to one of the selected restaurants, I came upon a blackboard special that offered lamb shanks at a very low price. I could not resist and so added another excellent restaurant to my list. They had an extensive beer offering and lunch became a tasting.

Brauhaus Füssen has a line that includes **FÜSSENER EDEL PILS**, a brilliant deep gold, with a light hop nose, bright crisp hop flavor, malt finish and a long pleasing aftertaste; **FÜSSENER FEST BOCK** was medium deep brown color, had a malt nose and very rich malt flavor, big body, smooth, a long rich malt aftertaste, very delicious and alcoholic (7.25%); and **FÜSSENER EXPORT**, a tawny-gold beer with a light malt and hop aroma, a palate with plenty of hops in front that got maltier from the middle on, good balance, good body and a long malt aftertaste. It was good but lacked the crispness of the Pils. The Fest Bock was good enough for seconds. They also had the beers of **Allgäuer Brauhaus**, a brewery in Kempten, a larger town about twenty miles away. These brews were **ALT KEMPTENER WEISSE DUNKEL** — deep cloudy brown, terrific appetizing wheat and barley malt nose, zesty tangy flavor is smooth and drinkable, good body, great character, long long malt aftertaste; **ALLGÄUER BRAUHAUS URTYP EXPORT** — gold, faint hop and malt nose, dull malt flavor, dry hop aftertaste, medium length; **ALLGÄUER BRAUHAUS DAS HELLE** — gold, very faint hop nose, hop and malt flavor, not in balance, dry hop aftertaste, medium length; **ALLGÄUER BRAUHAUS FÜRSTADT WEIZEN**—cloudy gold, big bright spicy nose, creamy, good malt and clove flavor, balanced, the malt softens the spicy nature, long aftertaste like the flavor; **ALLGÄUER BRAUHAUS EDELBRÄU** — gold, big malt nose, strong malt flavor, tasty lip-smacking sipping beer, big body, long dry malt aftertaste, excellent balance, excellent beer; and **TEUTSCH PILS** — gold, malt and light hop nose, flavor is malt first, thence big hops to the finish, long dry hop aftertaste.

Some of the other nearby towns with breweries were Kaufbeuren, whose **Brauerei Aktien** labels are now readily found in the U.S. and Marktoberdorf, home of **Brauerei Franz Josef Sailer,** whose Sailer and Oberdorfer labels have all been seen in the U.S. We saw nothing here that we had not already seen at home. Also in this area is **Irseer Kloster-brauerei** at Irseer. This is another attractive Privater Brauerei Gasthof with a hotel of 40 rooms, beer garden, restaurant, brewery, brewery-museum, academy and church. They make brandy, liqueur, wine and several beers. We were able to taste **IRSEER KLOSTER STARKBIER** — brownish amber, toasted malt nose, dry malt flavor, richer at the end than at the start, off-dry rich malt aftertaste is very long, excellent balance, a big beautiful strong brew.

Fully lunched and beered, Neuschwanstein and Hohenschwangau castles were next on the schedule, both of which require a lot of uphill walking. Neuschwanstein is the classic fairy tale castle, the inspiration for Disney's castle, only it is real and magnificent. The last of Mad Ludwig's building sprees, it broke the treasury of Bavaria and may have been the cause of his untimely demise, which occurred under strange circumstances. Because the construction went into overrun, the interior lacks the adornments of the other castles, but is reasonably complete, unlike the Herrenchiemsee (which, though somewhat outfitted is not complete). Hohenschwangau was his childhood home and residence of his parents. Hohenschwangau was originally a medieval fortress. For viewing treasures, this tiny castle is the place to go. It boggles the mind.

In Füssen were found some of the beers of **Privatbrauerei Johann Röck K.G.** of Nesselwang. They were **BÄREN PILS** — gold, hop aroma, mild malt-hop flavor, good body, very good balance, refreshing, complex, long dry hop aftertaste, a superb Pils; **BÄREN GOLD** — gold, light malt nose and flavor, well balanced, dry hop finish and long aftertaste, a delicate brew with great finesse; **BÄREN BRÄU ALT-BAYRISCH DUNKEL** — brown, nice malt aroma, dry rich clean malt flavor, medium long dry malt aftertaste; **BÄREN BRÄU ALPEN BOCK** — brown, rich malt nose has great complexity and earthiness, extremely big rich roasted malt flavor, has a nut-like quality, quite complex, long dry roasted malt aftertaste continues the nutty taste, a most satifying bock and one of the best found; and **BÄREN WEIZEN HEFETRUB** — hazy gold, clean zesty nose, nice mild malt taste, very drinkable, medium body, good balance, dies at the finish, very little aftertaste. The Pils, Gold and Alpen Bock are highly recommended.

The most direct route back was via Reutte and Lermoos, Austria. That shorter route avoids backtracking and gives the opportunity to pick up some 15-20 Austrian beers. I won't discuss them here, but they will be reported in the 1993 update to "The Beer Log."[1]

The next day the sun was shining brilliantly, good for climbing the Zugspitze, a mountain approximately 9,650 feet above sea level. It can be ascended via an electric cog railway or by cable car. If you take the Zugspitzbahn train to Eibsee, you can either continue on the train or transfer to the Eibseebahn cable car and go directly to the summit. We climbed it up in a cable car and from the summit descended on the Gipfelbahn cable car to Hotel Schneefernerhaus where you can catch the Zugspitzbahn train back down the mountain to your car park and do it all in the same day. There is also an ice tunnel that crosses the border to the customs point, the Zugspitzkamm, where another cable car, The Tiroler

Zugspitzbahn runs to Erwald Austria. The view from the train is spectacular and, from the cable cars, breathtaking. You will rarely find a more pleasant adventure. If you are a skier, there is a full day of great sport awaiting you as well.

The day gave us little beer tasting (there is beer served on the mountain, to be sure), but tomorrow we planned a visit to Munich and knew we could make up for it then. Nearby was lovely Mittenwald, which offers pretty much all you could want of a town in the Alps and less tourists than most, including a fantastic cable car ride up the Karwendl, a mountain 2,000 feet shorter than the Zugspitze, but no less thrilling. Mittenwald's brewery is **Privatbrauerei Mittenwalder** with a product line comprised of **MITTENWALDER DUNKEL** a deep ruby-brown brew with a lovely malt nose and flavor, magnificent balance and long malt aftertaste, a very pleasant and satisfying beer; **MITTENWALDER WEIHNACHTSBOCK HELL** was a bit sour and probably too old or mistreated; **MITTENWALDER JOSEFI BOCK DUNKEL** was deep ruby-brown, had a rich malt nose and off-dry malt flavor and long malt aftertaste, a good drinkable brew; and **MITTENWALDER VOLLBIER HELL** a golden brew with a malt and faint hop aroma, a malt flavor that is off-dry and a little vegetal at first but becomes drier toward the finish, light dry malt aftertaste and is overall somewhat dull.

Our drive to Munich started out in rain. This soon turned to light snow and alternated between snow and rain for the better part of two hours. We travelled slowly, hoping the weather would improve, stopping at nearby Holzkirchen to pick up some of their local beers. **Privatbrauerei Oberäu Wochinger K.G.** is the brewery. Their beers are **HOLZKIRCHNER OBERÄU PILS** — gold, hop nose, big hop flavor, well backed with malt, highly carbonated, good body, long dry malt and hop aftertaste; **HOLZKIRCHNER OBERÄU EDEL EXPORT** — very deep gold, faint malt nose, fairly big malt flavor, big body, long malt aftertaste; **HOCHLAND HELL** — gold, malt-hop nose and flavor, off-dry malt finish, long drier malt aftertaste; **HOLZKIRCHNER OBERÄU URTYP HELL** — gold, malt and hop aroma, flavor is mostly malt with some hops in back, dry malt-hop finish and long dry hop aftertaste; **HOLZKIRCHNER WEISSE DUNKEL** — deep amber-brown, citrus lemony-grapefruit malt nose, creamy, light spicy clove and malt flavor, dry malt finish, long dry malt aftertaste shows little of the spiciness; **HOLZKIRCHNER WEISSE BAYERISCHES HEFEWEIZEN** — hazy gold, faint lactic spice in behind a malt aroma, mild spicy flavor, medium body, long mild spice and malt aftertaste; and **HOLZKIRCHNER LAURENZI EXPORT DUNKEL** — good deep brown, roasted malt nose, rich roasted malt flavor, finishes dry, long dry malt aftertaste, medium body, good balance.

A bit closer to Munich is Aying and the Brauerei Gasthof Hotel Aying, more familiar to Americans as Privatbrauerei Franz Inselkammer. This brewery's products (the Ayinger beers and Celebrator Doppelbock) are imported by Merchant du Vin. All the beers we could find have been seen regularly back home, but it should be noted that this is a most attractive brewery hotel only some 25 km from Munich.

As a tourist stop, Munich is a very large cosmopolitan city with great shopping sections, many old buildings and churches, some of Germany's finest museums and a great beer tradition. During Oktoberfest (which comes in late September), it is almost impossible to find lodgings. The fest is easily accomplished by parking far from the grounds but near a subway entrance and taking public transportation directly to the location, which is at a large fairgrounds called the Theresienwiese. Finding a seat inside one of the large fest halls is another problem. It is the biggest carnival in the world. I have been to it four times and never tire of the excitement and fun it offers. There is plenty of great beer, too. When the fest is not on, you can still catch a lot of the beery excitement for each of the major Munich breweries operates a beer hall and there are numerous beer gardens where you can wet your whistle. The bigger ones put on entertainment quite similar to that offered during the fest. It is just a lot smaller and less well attended. Actually, it is a lot easier to crawl from one beer hall to another in the city than it is to get from one hall to another at the Oktoberfest, even though they are closer together at the fest. That is because the fest is so very crowded. Had the Oktoberfest been in

Hofbräuhaus Munich.

39

progress, we would have spent the day there. Since it was months away, we went from one beer hall to another in the vast downtown area, stopping off in between to view the interior of churches, spend some time in the museums and just walk the streets taking in the sights and the people. I find it unrewarding to drive in this sprawling city, so I park at some convenient stop near public transportation and use my feet and the MVV. The Münchner Verkehrs und Tarifverbund (MVV, for short) is inexpensive, dependable, and easy to use. There are surface and underground means and very clear maps and signs. A day ticket (Tageskarte) costs less than $5.

We tasted all our old Munich favorites on draft, enjoying the pils at the Hofbrauhaus in great litre sized *krugs,* sipping Animator at Hacker-Pschorr, marveling over Maximator at Augustiner, and indulging ourselves with Paulaner's Salvator. For those who don't know, any German beer ending in -ator is a double bock. There are dozens of them, almost all worth finding to collect in your memories. Two of the major brewers have beer hall-restaurants on Neuhauser Str. (Augustiner, Hacker-Pschorr) and there are Löwenbräu (Bayern Str.) and Spaten nearby. The Hofbrauhaus is only a short walk from the Residenz, one of Munich's most famous tourist attractions in the downtown center area. The best of the Munich beer gardens is described in a useful book, "The Beer Drinker's Guide to Munich," by Larry Hawthorne.[2] If you are going to spend any length of time in Munich drinking beer, I recommend this book because it gives in-depth descriptions, thorough directions and hours of operation. His list of the best very nearly coincides with mine and I offer it here with addresses and brewery affiliations:

ALTES HACKERHAUS Sendlinger Str. 75 (Hacker-Pschorr)
AM HOPFENGARTEN Siegenburger Str. 43 (Löwenbräu)
AM ROSENGARTEN Westendstrasse 305 (Paulaner)
AUGUSTINER GROSSGASTSTÄTTE Neuhauser Str 16 (Augustiner)
AUGUSTINER KELLER Arnulfstrasse 52 (Augustiner)
BRÜCKENWIRT An der Grunwalder Brücke 1 (Löwenbräu)
DEUTSCHE EICHE Ranerstrasse 1 (Maisacher Bräu)
ENGLISCHER GARTEN — Four beer gardens in a park as follows:
    CHINESISCHER TURM Englischer Garten 3 (Löwenbräu)
    SEEHAUS Kleinhesselohe 3 (Paulaner)
    HIRSCHAU Gyslingstrasse 15 (Spaten)
    ZUM AUMEISTER Sondermeierstrasse 1 (Hofbrauhaus)
ZUM FLAUCHER Isarauen 1 (Löwenbräu)
FORSCHUNGSBRAUEREI (Experimental Brewery) Unterhachinger Str 76
HARLICHINGER EINKEHR Karolinger Allee 34 (Löwenbräu)
HAUS DER 111 BIERE Franz Str 3 (111 different brands, 8 on tap)
GASTHOF HINTERBRÜHL Hinterbrühl 2 (Löwenbräu)
HIRSCHGARTEN Hirschgarten 1 (Augustiner)
HOFBRAUHAUS Am Platzl/Orlando Str near Marienplatz (Hofbrauhaus)
HOFBRAU KELLER Am Wiener Platz Haidhausen (Hofbrauhaus)
IM GRÜNTAL Im Grüntal 7 (Paulaner)
LEIBERHEIM Nixenweg 9 (Erhartinger Bräu)
LÖWENBRÄU KELLER Nymphenburger Str 2 (Löwenbräu)
MANGOSTIN ASIA Maria Einsiedel Str 2 (Löwenbräu)
MATHÄSER BIER STADT Bayer Str. 5 (Löwenbräu)
MAX EMANUEL BRAUEREI Adalbertstrasse 33 (Löwenbräu)
MENTERSCHWAIGE Menterschwaigstrasse 4 (Löwenbräu)
MICHAELIGARTEN Feichtstrasse 10 (Löwenbräu)
PARK CAFE Sophienstrasse 7 (Löwenbräu)

SALVATOR KELLER Hochstrasse 77 (Paulaner)
SANKT EMMERAMS MÜHLE St. Emmeram 41 (Spaten)
SCHIESS STÄTTE Zielstattstrasse 6 (Kaltenberger Bräu)
SIEBENBRUNN Siebenbrunner Str 5 (Spaten)
TANNENGARTEN Pfeuferstrasse 32 (Hacker-Pschorr)
TAXISGARTEN Taxis Str 1 (Spaten)
BIERGARTEN VIKTUALIENMARKT Am Vicktualienmarkt (6 Munich beers)
WALDHEIM Zum Waldheim 1 (Hacker-Pschorr)
WALDWIRTSCHAFT GROSSHESSELOHE George Kalb Str 3 in
    Grosshesselohe (Spaten) (*Note:* There is a microbrewery [Isar Bräu] in the
    Grosshesselohe Isartal Bahnhof (station).
WEISSES BRÄUHAUS Tal Str 10 (Schneider Weisse/ Karmelitan Kloster)

Lunchtime entertainment at Hofbrauhaus Munich.

    We had a fine day, but when it was over I found I had taken notes on only the first two beers of the day, at **Hofbrauhaus München** noting **HOFBRÄUHAUS MÜNCHEN HELL** — gold, marvelous hop and malt aroma, flavor to match, big and bright, complex and very well-balanced, long medium dry hop aftertaste, very drinkable and great with food, and **HOFBRÄUHAUS MÜNCHEN DUNKEL** — dark amber-brown, rich lightly toasted malt nose, flavor to match the nose, good body, fine balance, very drinkable, long dry malt aftertaste with the hops way in back but contributing to the balance, very good with German wursts. Each was a full litre and that killed my pen for several hours.

    There are plenty of tourist attractions in Munich, most easily reached on foot. There is the Marienplatz in the center of the city with the Rathaus Carillon playing at 11 am and noon. There is also the very famous Residenzmuseum, the Frauenkirche (which is always shown on Munich travel posters and is the dominant visual feature seen when approaching Munich), the Münchener Stadtmuseum, and a considerable number of lesser museums and churches.

    Easing out of Munich at the end of the day, we did stop at a few getränkmarkts to see what new beers might be found. In Munich, though, you mostly find only Munich beers, but that is not bad. There are many that have never seen our shores and they are well worth finding. **Brauerei Löwenbräu**, whose great pils was once a treasure on our store shelves until Miller gained the rights to produce it in the U.S., makes a number of excellent beers that are not exported here. **LÖWENBRÄU OKTO-BERFEST**, as served at the festhalle is brilliant deep gold, has a dense head that lasts all the way to the bottom of the glass, has a balanced malt and hop nose, delicious rich malt flavor well backed with hops, big body, and a long delicious dry hop aftertaste. In the bottle it is still good, but different. It is deep amber, has a lovely dry hop nose, smooth balanced hop and malt palate, and is very drinkable and fairly long on the palate. **DER LÖWENBRÄU PREMIUM PILSENER** is pale gold, has a nice thick head, clean hop nose, big fresh hop and malt flavor, creamy texture, and a delicious complex long dry hop aftertaste. The balance is excellent throughout. **LÖWEN WEISSE KLARES WEIZENBIER** is bright clear gold with a big head, pleasant clean off-dry malt nose, pleasant slightly sweet malt flavor with just a little lactic tang, really good balance, and a long pleasing aftertaste like the flavor. **TRIUMPHATOR DUNKLER DOPPELBOCK** is deep red-brown with a roasted malt aroma that is complex and rich, big rich malt flavor is on the sweet side in front, dry at the middle, long medium dry malt aftertaste, and is very complex and very good. **LÖWENBRÄU HELLER BOCK** is brilliant gold, has a beautiful hop nose, big bright malt flavor, is strong, rich, and complex, has a full body, and a long malt and hop aftertaste, with hops coming on strongly at the very end. **LÖWENBRÄU SCHWARZE-WEISSE DUNKLES HEFE-WEIZEN** is slightly hazy deep copper-amber, has a wheat and malt aroma with a faint lactic acid character like clove spice, palate to match, nicely balanced, smooth, well-made, and very drinkable. **LÖWENBRÄU BOCKBIER HELL** is deep gold, has a fragrant hop nose, big hop and malt flavor, big body, finishes dry hops, and an aftertaste of dry hops and malt. This is a beer with plenty of everything including an excellent balance. Even the Löwenbräu non-alcoholic brew is excellent.

Zum Pschorrbräu in Munich.

The only new beer we found from **Augustiner Bräu** was **AUGUSTINER BRÄU MÜNCHEN OKTOBERFEST BIER** — bright gold, slightly off-dry malt aroma, very well-balanced malt and hop flavor, big body, alcohol seems high, very long slightly sour hop aftertaste, smooth and flavorful beer with good balance.

From **Hacker-Pschorr** there was **HACKER-PSCHORR HUBERTUS BOCK** — deep gold, huge off-dry malt nose, big, smooth, rich, balanced clean malt flavor, high alcohol (6.8%), finely carbonated, very drinkable despite its heft, long rich malt aftertaste, a super beer.

Augustiner Grossgaststätte in Munich.

From **Hofbräuhaus München** we found these three: **HOFBRÄU MÜNCHEN ROYAL EXPORT HELL** — bright gold, fragrant roasted malt and hop aroma, delicious and complex malt and hop flavor, excellent balance, long and dry, good body, a brightly flavored good tasting brew; **HOFBRÄUHAUS MÜNCHEN DELICATOR** — deep amber, light malt aroma, big dry malt flavor, big body, long dry malt aftertaste, a solid doublebock; and **HOFBRÄUHAUS MÜNCHEN BOCK HELL** — gold, great malt-hop aroma, huge hop and malt flavor, malt is a bit toasted, great balance, huge body, high density (16.3°), high alcohol (6.7%), delicious, long dry malt and hop aftertaste much like the flavor.

A single new item appeared from **Paulaner, PAULANER MÜNCHENER UR-BOCK HELL** — amber-gold, toasted malt and hop aroma, medium body, good tasting toasted malt and hop flavor, bright and hoppy up front, rich toasted malt at the finish, complex, balanced, long toasted malt aftertaste.

Many **Spaten** brews were seen, but none of them new to us. We must have access to most of them in the U.S. according to what we observed. We did find two brews from **G. Schneider & Sohn K.G./Brauerei Kelheim**, a wheat beer brewery that was located in Munich until after WWII, at which time it moved to Kelheim (near Regensburg). **SCHNEIDER WEISSE HEFE-WEIZENBIER** was hazy amber, had a nose that was lightly lactic but mostly pleasant malt, a mellow and smooth flavor, good balance, a sour finish shows the lactic acid and spice promised by the nose, and a long faintly sour aftertaste. **AVENTIUS WEIZENSTARKBIER** was hazy deep copper color with a huge dense head, delightful appetizing malt-wheat-lightly lactic nose, big off-dry malt and lactic acid/spicy flavor, high alcohol, big body, heavy flavor, extremely tasty and balanced, with a very long complex aftertaste like the flavor. It is a dandy weizenbier, perhaps the best I ever tasted from a bottle. Swinging around Munich, we picked up a pair from a small private brewery, **Privatbrauerei Schweiger** in Markt Schwaben bei München. Their beers were **SCHWEIGER HELLES EXPORT** — gold, malt nose, malt flavor with good hop support, off-dry hop finish,

43

good body, good balance, hop aftertaste is similar to finish but drier, fairly long, and **SCHWEIGER SCHMANKERL WEISSE** — very slightly hazy gold, faint spicy nose, bright clove flavor, finish, and aftertaste, short, but good while it lasts. Another small brewery find was the **Wildbräu Brewery** in Grafing with **LANDPILS NACH ALTER BRÄUHERRN ART**, a pale golden beer with a light hop aroma, mild hop flavor, and a long dry sour hop aftertaste. Another small brewery found was **Schlossbrauerei Hohenkammer** in Hohenkamm. The two beers found were **HOHENKAMMER WEISSE** — hazy gold, pleasant complex spicy-berry peach fruit nose, complex flavor with malt, spice, and fruit, creamy, light body, sags a bit at the finish, fruity aftertaste and **HOHENKAMMER SCHLOSSBIER SCHLOSS-BRÄU HELL** — very deep gold, hop nose, good hop and malt flavor, highly carbonated, dry malt finish and aftertaste. A visit to the Forschungs Brewery, the house-brewery or brewpub in the suburb of Perlach, was planned but time did not permit its inclusion. Their St. Jacobus bock beer is highly reputed.

We could have easily spent a week in Munich quite profitably, but regrettably wished to get much further into the boondocks, away from the familiar, away from the well beaten tourist tracks. We were ready to head to the Bömischewald, the forested area along the Czech border.

---

[1] *The Beer Log* by James D. Robertson, published by Bosak Publishing, Inc., 4764 Galicia Way, Oceanside, CA 92056. $37.50 + S/H. *1993 Update to The Beer Log*, Sections 1 & 2; $10 ea. or $16/both + S/H.

[2] *The Beer Drinker's Guide to Munich* by Larry Hawthorne, published by Freizeit Publishers, 377 Keahole St., Suite 6-265, Honolulu, HI 96825. $8.95

Nights in The Bömischewald

Since we were housed on the southwest side of Munich, we had to pass Munich again the next day on our eastward course. This was not by accident, for there are many breweries to the east of that great beer city and we hoped to stop off at such towns as Freising and Erding. **Bayerische Staatsbrauerei Weihenstephan** is a huge brewery, school and yeast manufacturing facility in Freising, operated by the Bavarian government. It has been operating since 1040 and lays claim to be the oldest operating brewery in the world. They maintain strains of yeast for breweries all over the country and export to the world. The school is world famous and many American brewmasters go there for education and refresher courses as they also operate a research facility constantly developing new techniques. We had hoped to take a tour but the weather did not cooperate and the rains fell in a torrent. With many miles to travel in adverse conditions, we decided to forego this plan and just settle for some of the beer for tasting. They do make nine different types of excellent brew, all of which are available for sampling at their *Bräustüberl* (Beer garden and restaurant). **VITUS WEIZENBOCK** is a pale amber wheat beer with a pleasant malt-wheat nose that has a faint trace of lactic spice, good flavor much like the aroma with a hint of sweetness, balanced, complex, pleasant and refreshing and a medium long aftertaste like the flavor, but drier. The **WEIHENSTEPHAN KORBINIAN DUNKLES STARKBIER** is amber-brown, has a malt nose, good body, rich malt flavor, dry hop finish, very good balance and a long dry hop aftertaste. It is very satisfying. **WEIHENSTEPHAN WEIZENBIER KRISTALL EXPORT** is bright gold with a big head, fresh grainy wheat and barley malt aroma, quite fresh and zesty, very little acid

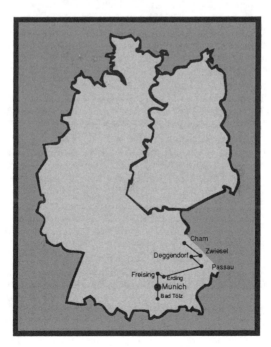

in the malt flavor but enough for character and a long malt aftertaste. It is bright, pleasant, refreshing and very drinkable. Recently arrived in the U.S., this brew is labelled **WEIHENSTEPHAN WEIZENBIER CRYSTAL CLEAR. WEIHENSTEPHAN HEFE-WEISSBIER** is hazy gold, has a lactic spicy clove nose, flavorful zesty clove flavor, spice strong in front, eases off in mid-palate enough for smooth slightly off-dry malt to rise up, finish and aftertaste are off-dry malt, with the spicy cloves coming again very late in the long aftertaste. **STEPHAN-SQUELL HELLES STARKBIER** is medium deep gold, with a very rich malt aroma, huge malty flavor (like malted milk powder), a bit wine-like but has a good balance and a long dry malt aftertaste. In the U.S. market, this brew is called **WEIHENSTEPHAN ORIGINAL.**

Another brewery in Freising is **Hofbrauhaus Moy.** They offer **HOFBRAUHAUS MOY JÄGERBIER** — bright gold, light off-sweet nose with hops in back, good smooth delicate malt and hop flavor, finely balanced, slightly sweet malt aftertaste, a nice silky smooth brew, **HOFBRAUHAUS MOY REGENT** — bright gold, dry complex malt nose with a little ale-like tartness, good smooth delicate taste similar to above but with more hops in front, long dry hop aftertaste and **HOF-BRAUHAUS MOY EDELWEIZEN KRISTALLKLAR** — bright gold, big head, clean wheat nose, zesty clean wheat and malt flavor, tastes good, good body, slightly sweet finish and aftertaste, medium to short duration.

In nearby Erding is the **Brauerei Brombach, Erdinger Weissbräu,** one of the major weizenbier breweries in Bavaria. We searched high and low, but could find no labels not already seen in the USA. Frankenmuth B.C. is presently importing these fine beers and apparently is doing a complete job. Another prolific brewery is **Klosterbrauerei Scheyern** at Scheyern, which does not export its beers. Their lineup consists of: **KLOSTERBRAUEREI SCHEYERN DUNKLER KLOSTER-BOCK** — deep amber-brown, light dry malt aroma, dry malt flavor, long pleasant off-dry malt aftertaste which gets a bit sweeter at the end, medium duration, very drinkable; **KLOSTERBRAUEREI SCHEY-ERN KLOSTER-DOPPELBOCK DUNKEL** — deep brown, some-what stinky-earthy roasted malt aroma, big dry roasted malt flavor, extremely rich and yet surprisingly dry, lush yet smooth, very long dry malt aftertaste, has great subtlety, a marvelous brew despite the offish start and the 7.3% alcohol, which is barely noticeable; **KLOSTER-BRAUEREI SCHEYERN KLOSTER-GOLD** — gold, fragrant hop nose, sweet hop flavor, good body, fair balance, long dry hop aftertaste; **KLOSTERBRAUEREI SCHEYERN KLOSTER-WEISSE HELL** — hazy gold, big head, grapefruit-like aroma, vegetal-grapefruit flavor, long dry malt aftertaste; and **KLOSTERBRAUEREI SCHEYERN KLOSTER-WEISSE DUNKEL** — hazy brown, nose of cloves, candy and fruit, strong spicy-candy flavor, very assertive, flavor carries into the long aftertaste.

Also located in Erding is the **Stiftungsbrauere,** maker of **DIE SCHWARZE DUNKLES WEISSBIER** — brown, malt nose with a lactic-spice background, flavor like the nose but even spicier, dry malt finish and aftertaste.

Another of the small breweries found in the region just to the east of Munich is **Privatbrauerei Hellbräu Altöttinger** in Altötting with **ALTÖTTINGER FEIN HERB HELL-BRÄU** — gold, malt aroma, pleasant malty flavor, lightly hopped, dry malt and light hop aftertaste and **ALTÖTTINGER BAYRISCH DUNKEL** — deep brown, big off-dry grainy malt nose, rich malt flavor is also grainy, big body, good balance, delicious, off-dry malt finish, long dry malt aftertaste, good complexity and very drinkable, excellent dark pils.

Continuing eastward, there are small brewery marketing areas, one after another. One notable brewery is **Privatbrauerei Röhrl** in Frontenhausen. They make **RÖHRL EXPORT BEER** — gold, hop nose, hop flavor with plenty of malt, long bright malt aftertaste, balanced and bright, good tasting brew and **RÖHRL VILSTALER DUNKLES HEFE-WEIZEN** — deep brown, very clear with all the yeast in the bottom, big malt nose, delicate spicy malt flavor, smooth and tasty, rich malt finish, long dry malt aftertaste, an excellent hefe-weizen.

Driving through this area named Hallertau means passing through miles and miles of hop fields. When in season the hop vines soar into the air on lines held aloft by long poles. Out of season, the land seems to be a barren waste, sometimes with the empty poles left to puzzle passing tourists. As we neared the autobahn that runs between Passau and Regensburg (and separates the rolling hills of the hop fields from the eastern mountains and forests), the area becomes more populated and more likely as a territory for finding beer. Our destination was Zwiesel, a somewhat remote town only minutes from the border of Czechoslovakia in the *Böhmischewald* (Bohemian forest), a town with a brewery-hotel. The distance from the autobahn was only 30 miles as the crow flies, so we had ample time to putter about visiting getränkmarkts, supermarkets and gasthofs finding the local beers. Also, the weather had become more accommodating to wandering about town on foot.

In elegant Passau with its Baroque, Rococo and Neoclassical facades crowded together on a narrow peninsula on the confluence of the Danube and Inn Rivers, there was **Traditionsbrauerei Harklberg** with **HARKLBERG HOCHFÜRST PILSENER** — gold, fresh hop nose, hop flavor is a little sour, especially at the finish, dull aftertaste; **HARKLBERG URHELL** — gold, stinky hop nose, zesty hop and malt flavor, flabby finish, dull aftertaste; **HARKLBERG JAKOBI WEIZEN** — cloudy gold, malt nose, light slightly fruity-spicy malt flavor, long dull dry malt aftertaste has cloves way in back, medium body, not balanced; and **HARKLBERG JAKOBI DUNKLE WEISSE** — hazy brown, huge dense head like a fass (draft) beer, smooth spicy malt nose, fresh lightly spiced malty-fruity flavor, good body, slightly spicy malt finish, long dry malt and hop aftertaste, good tasting satisfying brew. Also in the Passau area was **Brauerei Aldersbach/ Frhr v. Aretin, K.G.** in Aldersbach with **ALDERSBACHER KLOSTER HELL** — gold, malt and hop aroma, very light malt flavor and finish, weak malt aftertaste and **ALDERSBACHER DUNKEL HEFE-WEIZEN** — deep amber-brown, nice spicy hop and malt nose, bright fruity-spicy malt flavor, long dry malt aftertaste with the fruit and spice way in back, a tangy, tasty, drinkable beer.

A short distance away was **Wolfstetter Bräu George Huber** in Vilshofen who makes **WOLFSTETTER VOLLBIER HELL** — gold, sour hop nose, very sour hop taste, dry hop finish and aftertaste; **WOLFSTETTER HERREN PILS** — gold, zesty hop nose, malt flavor with a hop finish, long dry hop aftertaste; **WOLFSTETTER EXPORT HEFE-WEIZEN** — hazy gold, pleasant spicy malt nose, big spicy malt flavor, huge palate, big body, has to be taken in small sips, no guzzling this one, spicy malt finish and aftertaste, a brute of a beer; and **WOLFSTETTER RATSHERREN WEISSBIER** — brown, pleasant spicy malt aroma, creamy malt and spicy cloves on the palate, fairly big, good body, smooth and creamy, dry malt finish and aftertaste.

Nearby we found **Arcobräu, Grafliches Brauhaus,** a brewery in Moos. The labels found were: **ARCOBRÄU MOOSER HELL** — brilliant clear gold, big hop nose, balanced hop and malt flavor, good body, dry malt finish and aftertaste; **ARCOBRÄU PILSENER** — pale gold, clean hop nose, big hop flavor in front, malt in middle, dry hop finish, long dry hop aftertaste, good body, fairly complex, good balance; **ARCOBRÄU URWEISSE** — hazy gold, bright hop nose, big spicy clove, hop and malt flavor, very smooth, good body, light spicy finish, long spicy malt aftertaste; and **GRAF ARCO GRAFEN HELL** — gold, lovely malt and hop nose, zesty fresh flavor, big malt finish, long malt aftertaste with plenty of good hop support. The origin of this bottle was Grafliches Brauereien Arco, Adldorf, but we could not find Adldorf on any map. Recently, two brews from this brewery have appeared in the USA and they are described as follows for comparison with the above: **COUNT ARCO'S BAVARIAN WEISSBIER WITH YEAST** — gold, spicy lactic nose, pleasant spicy flavor with off-dry wheat in back, good mouth feel, short dry spicy malt aftertaste; and **COUNT ARCO'S BAVARIAN FESTBIER** — gold, beautiful fresh rising malt aroma, fresh creamy medium dry malt flavor, good body, very drinkable, long medium dry lightly toasted malt aftertaste.

At Deggendorf, just off the autobahn on the way to Zwiesel we found one beer from **Weizenbrauerei Deggendorf,** the only one seen in the town. It was **BAYER WEIZEN** — hazy amber, big spicy-fruity malt nose and flavor, dry malt finish, fruit and spice return for the long aftertaste, good tasting brew. Plan to visit Deggendorf at the end of July-early August when they hold a *Volkfest* (although that translates to folk fest, read that as beer-festival). Other than that, the tour books recommend the area only for hiking and I must admit the forests are gorgeous for that purpose.

The road from Deggendorf to Zwiesel is full of twists and turns, steep hills and sudden drop-offs, a slow trip through some beautiful forests with occasional distant views of the mountains and cultivated valleys. It is a very rural area and is not greatly different in appearance from the western edge of Czechoslovakia that it borders. Zweisel itself has a main drag that is a steep hill, with our destination, **Privater Brauerei Gasthof Deutscher Rhein/Jankåbräu BRD**, near the top. This brewery-Gasthof has 25 rooms, a restaurant featuring wild game and *Böhmische* (Bohemian) specialties, zither music, Röck's Bärwurz (a honey based liqueur with forest herbs) and a good selection of beer from their brewery. With our game supper we tasted **JANKÅBRÄU BÖHMISCHES BOHEME** — gold, smooth pleasant hop nose and taste, plenty of supporting malt, long dry malt and hop aftertaste, a good tasting refreshing pils, **JANKÅBRÄU BÖHMISCHES KUPFER SPEZIAL** — brown, light malt nose and flavor, good body, long dry malt aftertaste and **JANKÅBRÄU BÖHMISCHES SCHWARZESWEIZEN** — dark brown, big tan head, typical rich spicy malt aroma and taste, good body, good balance, flavorful, long malt aftertaste.

Privater Brauerei Gasthof Deutscher Rhein in Zwiesel.

Our supper and beer left us in need of a walk, so we headed off down the hill to see what might be open, or just to look in shop windows. Only a few steps down the hill we ran into a brew-pub, **Dampfbierbrauerei Zwiesel - W. Pfeffer**. We were intrigued by the name since Dampfbier means steam beer, according to a translation I once received with regard to a Brauerei Maisel product some years back. There was no one there who could explain to us what *they* meant by steam beer so we had to content ourselves with tasting the beer. **PFEFFERBRÄU ZWIESEL SPEZIAL PILSENER** was a golden brew with a big aromatic hop nose, smooth malt flavor that finishes weakly and a pleasant dry malt aftertaste. **PFEFFERBRÄU MÄRZENBIER** was amber with a hop and malt aroma, spicy hop and malt flavor (more herbal than spice actually), low carbonation and a dry spicy finish and aftertaste. Our walk didn't help, so we went back to our hotel, had another beer or two and packed it in.

The sun was shining brightly the next morning and we continued wandering about the Bohemian Forest, looking for obscure beers. A delightful find was **Privaterbrauereigasthof Eck**, a brewery Gasthof in Böbrach-Eck. This place has been around (in one form or another) for about 500 years. Today it is a brewery with 22 guest rooms, a restaurant that features Bavarian-Bohemian specialties and a number of good brews. **ECKER BRÄU WILDERER DUNKEL** is brown, has a light roasted malt nose, off-dry malt front palate, dry malt middle and finish, good body, good balance and a long dry malt aftertaste. It is smooth, drinkable and has zest. **ECKER BRÄU EDEL PILS** is deep gold, has a fragrant hop aroma, complex rich hop and malt flavor, good body, complex dry hop and malt finish and aftertaste and is long and very good, an excellent brew. **ECKER BRÄU FAHNDERL-WEISSE HEFE-WEISSBIER** is bright clear gold, has a lovely light clove aroma, light clove and malt flavor, balanced, smooth, clean and has a dry malt finish and aftertaste. **ECKER BRÄU VOLLBIER HELL** is brilliant gold with a roasted caramel malt nose, smooth light roasted malt flavor and medium to long dry malt aftertaste. It is a very likeable beer. We considered it one of our better finds.

From Teisnach we picked up a single beer from **Ettl Bräu**. **ETTL-HELL** was a golden beer with a malt nose and flavor and somewhat flabby medium long malt aftertaste. It was malt all the way through and could have used a greater hop presence

We also located the **Spath Bräu** brewery in Lohberg am Ossen with **OSSER HELL** — gold hop nose, big malt flavor, malt finish, long dry malt aftertaste, good body and balance, **OSSER GOLD** — deep gold, malt aroma and big malt flavor, long malt aftertaste, hops very light throughout, but a nicely made pleasant tasting brew and **OSSER WEISSE (MIT SEINER HEFE)** — clear gold, light aroma of hops and spicy cloves, zesty clove flavor, very sparkly and creamy, refreshing, finishes with the spice leading the flavor into a lightly spiced malt aftertaste with good duration. *Mit Seiner Hefe* translates to "with its yeast," meaning that the yeast has not been filtered out i.e., a hefe-weizen.

Near the edge of the forest is the small city of Cham, home of **Hofmark Spezialitäten Brauerei.** Most of the Hofmark beers are exported to the USA, but one thing to remember is that they put on a big festival each year in May. Michael Jackson's video series briefly visited that fest. We were not present for the festival, nor did we find Hofmark beers different from that available in the USA. For tourists visiting the nearby town of Furth im Wald on the second and third Sundays in August, there is the opportunity to attend a great Bavarian festival, the *Drachenstich* which deals with St. George killing the *Drachen*. If you aren't into dragon slaying, there are plenty of beer tents.

Some small town breweries found in the vicinity of Cham were **Schloss Bräu** in Stamsried with its **HERZOG PILSENER**—gold, hop nose with a meaty background, big malt and hop flavor, finishes weakly, medium length dry hop aftertaste; **Brauerei Jacob** in Bodenwöhr with

BODENWÖR-HER JACOB ALTBAY-ERISCH HELL — gold, malt nose, good body, dry malt flavor, finish and aftertaste; and **Privatbrauerei Frank**, Neunburg, with **NEUN-BURGER WEIZEN HEFE-TRÜB** — hazy gold, lightly spiced malt aroma, good bright spicy malt flavor, finish and light aftertaste.

The Fränkische Alb

Heading back to the autobahn that runs from Passau to Frankfurt through Nürnberg and Würzburg, we landed at Regensburg, a beautiful city on the Danube with visible medieval roots and home to several well-known breweries. The city is easy to explore on foot with over a thousand buildings of historical interest crowded into a small area. Among worthwhile items to see is the 12th century stone bridge across the Danube, the Domstadt — a collection of eccelesiastical buildings built from 1250-1525, Stadtmuseum, merchants quarter, Schloss Thurn und Taxis and, of course, the breweries and bier gartens.

The biggest of the local breweries is **Fürstliche Brauerei Thurn und Taxis**, belonging to the Thurn und Taxis family, generally accepted as being the richest family in Germany. Their extensive line includes: **THURN U TAXIS HEFEWEIZEN** — cloudy amber, sweet wheaty weizen nose, much sweeter than usual for a wheat beer, spicy-fruity palate, complex, long off-dry malt aftertaste with only the faintest hint of cloves; **THURN U TAXIS POSTMEISTER DOPPELBOCK** — medium brown, big malt nose, strong malt flavor but very smooth, excellent balance, well rounded, quite long and very delicious; **SCHIERLINGEN ROGGEN OBERGÄRIG HEFETRUBE** —hazy deep amber, big head, sweet and sour lactic nose with a buttery background, buttery malt taste up front, lactic spice finish and aftertaste. Made for A.D. Laber Fürstliches Specialtätes-Brauhaus zu Schierling; **THURN U TAXIS DAS FURSTLICHE PILSENER** — gold, hop nose, hop flavor balanced well with malt, good body, long and strong dry hop aftertaste shows no malt whatever; and **THURN U TAXIS EXPORT** — gold, hop nose, good hefty hop and malt flavor, nicely balanced, big body, long malt aftertaste.

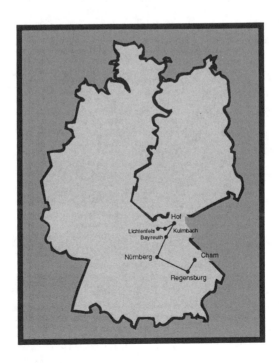

Another brewery in Regensburg is **Brauerei Bischofshof** with BISCHOFSHOF URHELL — gold, hop nose, pleasant bright hop flavor, good body, dry hop finish and long dry hop aftertaste and BISCHOFSHOF HEFE-WEISSBIER HELL — hazy gold, big spicy clove and malt aroma, creamy and refreshing, good body, spicy malt finish, long aftertaste is dry malt.

The best known *bier gartens* in town are Bischofshof (Am Dom), Kneitinger Garten (Müllerstr.), Kneitinger Keller (Galgenbergstr.) and Spitalgarten (Katharinenplatz).

Near to Regensburg is another brewery gasthof **Privatbrauereigasthof Prösslbräu** in Adlersberg. It is difficult to find although it is within sight of the Nittendorf exit off the autobahn between Nürnberg and Regensburg. One of their beers is truly great. It is **PRÖSSLBRÄU ADLERSBERG PALMATOR** — dark reddish-brown, has a chocolate malt nose that is smooth, a little smoky and faintly buttery, a very rich chocolate malt flavor, extremely rich yet dry, very complex, a big body and a long dry roasted malt aftertaste. The 6.3% alcohol is absorbed easily by the strength of the flavor and not even noticeable. The others are also good, but the Palmator is outstanding. **PRÖSSLBRÄU ADLERSBERG VOLLBIER DUNKEL** is deep red-brown, has a malt nose, very smooth rich dry malt flavor, good body and a long dry malt aftertaste. **PRÖSSLBRÄU ADLERSBERG KLOSTER-PILS** is gold, has a pleasant strong hop nose, big hop flavor and a long dry hop aftertaste. There are 13 rooms at Prösslbräu and a restaurant featuring local specialties.

There is also the **Riedenburger Brauhaus Michael Krieger K.G.** a brewery in Riedenburg with RIEDENBURGER WEIZEN — clear amber-gold, light spicy malt nose, clean creamy, spicy malt flavor, dry malt finish, faintly spicy long malt aftertaste. Another nearby brewery is **Landbrauerei Ludwig Erl** in Geiselhöring. They brew **ERL-HELL HELLES EXPORT BIER** — gold, big somewhat stinky hop nose, big hop flavor, good body, sour hop and off-dry malt aftertaste, poorly balanced.

Travelling about the region, a familiar building appeared (familiar from some beer labels) and did indeed turn out to be **Klosterbrauerei Weltenburg Gmbh.**, the monastery brewery at Weltenburg with some excellent brews. It is Bavaria's oldest monastery, most famous for its wonderful dark beers which it brews on premises and serves in its *Gaststätte*. **WELTENBURGER KLOSTER ASAM-BOCK** is its best (to my palate). A deep ruby-brown beer, it has an excellent earthy toasted malt nose, very complex palate of chocolate, acid, malt and hops, rich, big and gets better as it goes. The long medium dry malt aftertaste is interesting in itself considering the way the palate starts out, an absolutely delicious experience. The others are: **WELTENBURGER KLOSTER SPEZIAL DUNKEL** — amber-brown, big malt nose, rich malt flavor, light body, very little hops (if any), no complexity, medium to short aftertaste of malt with a bit of sourness at the end; **WELTEN-BURGER KLOSTER BAROCK DUNKEL** — deep rich amber, light toasted malt nose, smooth toasted malt flavor, good body, medium intensity, long light and dry malt aftertaste; and **WELTENBURGER KLOSTER HEFE-WEISSBIER DUNKEL** — deep amber, huge dense head, lactic clove spice nose, light clove and malt flavor, light body, medium long light dry aftertaste like the flavor, overall seems a bit puny, at least compared to other Weltenburger brews.

Nearby is an imposing edifice on a hill overlooking the Danube some 11 km east of Regensburg. It is Ludwig I's Walhalla monument modeled on the Parthenon. Although one could take issue with the concept, the site was well chosen and the word imposing is not used lightly.

Twenty km southwest of Regensburg is Kelheim, now home to the **George Schneider & Sohn** wheat beer brewery which was discussed earlier in the text dealing with Munich. We also found another Brauereigasthof, **Privater Brauereigasthof Schneider** in Essing, which we believe to be no relation to the George Schneider brewery. They have 20 rooms, a restaurant and some interesting beer: **JOS. SCHNEIDER MAIBOCK** — deep gold, hop nose, big hop taste with the malt in back, dry hop finish, long dry hop aftertaste, really good clean and bright flavor, good body and balance, very enjoyable; **JOS. SCHNEIDER MÄRZEN** — pale amber, hop nose, big hop and malt flavor, finishes dry, long dry hop and malt aftertaste, excellent balance, good body, a very fine brew; and **JOS. SCHNEIDER DUNKEL** — brown, malt aroma, rich straightforward malt palate, dry malt finish and long dry malt aftertaste, good body and balance, well-made beer.

In Ingolstadt, another of the ancient fortresses well worth visiting and the home of the Audi car factory, we found **Ingobräu** with **TILLY BRÄU HELL** — gold, vegetal hop nose and flavor, sour vegetal finish, dry hop aftertaste, not likeable (Note that the name Tilly comes from Field Marshal Johann Tilly, Ingolstadt's Catholic hero of the Thirty Years' War); and **Bürgerliches Brauhaus A.G.** with **AROMATOR DOPPELBOCK** — pale brown, sour malt aroma and flavor, big body, long malt aftertaste is drier and less sour than the flavor and **Brauerei Herrnbräu** with **MÖNSCHSHOF KAPUZINER WEISSE HEFETRÜB**, an amber brew with a lactic nose, off-sweet malt palate with acidic overtones that doesn't come off very well.

Arriving in Nürnberg, you quickly know that you are in Tucher and Patrizier country. Their beers were advertised everywhere. Nürnberg is also famous for Lebkuchen cookies, which meant Christmas in our house and a very old downtown section (*Altstadt*) with some of the best examples of Baroque architecture to be seen in Germany. We visited the old buildings and churches in the Altstadt walking streets that were old 500 years ago. The postwar reconstruction was done so well that it is hard to believe that this city was reduced to rubble in 1945. Highlights are the frauenkirche, Altes Rathaus, St. Sebaldus, Kaiserburg and the museums. For beers we looked for ones new to us, for **Tucher Bräu A.G.** does export many brands to the U.S. We found **TUCHER UBERSEE EXPORT BEER** — tawny-gold, malt aroma, medium body, very lightly dry toasted malt and hop flavor, dry slightly sour hop finish, light dry hop and toasted malt aftertaste; **BRÄUHAUS ROTHENBURG GERMAN PILSENER** — gold, light hop nose, harsh bitter hop flavor, sour metallic finish and aftertaste; **TUCHER WEIZEN** — bright deep gold, foamy, beautiful malt nose, zesty piquant flavor up front, dry very fresh and crisp wheaty middle, long clean off-dry malt finish and medium long aftertaste, a very fine brew that is a pleasure to drink; **TUCHER HEFE WEIZEN** — brilliant deep gold, foamy, good malt aroma with some wheat and yeast in back, piquant spicy flavor starts up front and stays throughout, a bit yeasty in the middle, slightly off-dry raspberry malt finish, medium long dry malt aftertaste keeps much of the piquancy of the flavor, very nicely done; **TUCHER HEFE-WEIZEN DUNKLES** — amber, malt nose, high carbonation, hop, spice and malt flavor (in that order), refreshing and drinkable, fairly light handed, short malt aftertaste; **TUCHER LORENZI BOCK HELL** — bright gold, malt and corn nose, toasted malt and corn flavor, finishes cleaner and better with just the malt, long dry malt aftertaste; **TUCHER MAIBOCK HELL** — deep gold, lovely toasted malt nose, big zesty hop and toasted malt flavor, fairly intense, very long aftertaste like the flavor, an excellent beer; **TUCHER FESTBIER MÄRZEN** — tawny-gold, pleasant toasted malt aroma, highly carbonated, good toasted malt flavor, sour hop aftertaste; **TUCHER BAJUVATOR DOPPELBOCK** — deep red-amber, roasted malt nose and taste, delicious, rich and clean, long roasted malt aftertaste is medium dry, very drinkable; **TUCHER BAYERISCHES WEISSBIER HEFE-WEIZEN** — tawny, faint citrus nose, spicy lactic flavor on front of the palate, medium dry malt in the middle and a touch of lactic with the malt in the finish, medium body, very brief dry malt aftertaste with no spice at all at the end; and **SEBALDUS WEIZENBOCK DUNKEL** — rich brown color, big creamy head and creamy texture, bright spicy clove aroma, zesty spicy rich malt flavor, complex and refreshing, long bright aftertaste like the flavor.

Since few of the beers of **Patrizier-Bräu, A.G.** reach the States, most of what was found were new: **PATRIZIER EXPORT** — deep amber, light hop nose, medium body, good malt flavor with the hops in back, long dry malt aftertaste; **PATRIZIER EDELHELL EXPORT** — bright gold, nice complex hop aroma, big hop flavor up front, malt shows through in the finish, good balance, very good taste, complex, softens and gets better as you sip, pleasant long malt aftertaste; **PATRIZIER PILS** — bright deep gold, toasted malt and hop aroma, light malt and hop palate, not exciting, brief malt aftertaste; **BAMBERGER HOFBRAU BEER** — tawny-gold, slightly off-dry malt and grain aroma, grainy slightly toasted palate, very light body, virtually no finish or aftertaste; **PATRIZIER POCULATOR** — pale brown, toasted malt aroma, intense dry malt flavor, big body, only medium duration but the feel of the strong flavor lasts in your mouth; and **PATRIZIER BRÄU KUPFESTUBE** — medium deep brilliant amber, toasted malt aroma and flavor, some smoke in the backtaste and in the finish, long toasted smoky malt aftertaste, very dry and very drinkable. **Lederer Bräu** is also located in Nürnberg, but we did not see any of their brands.

There is also the **Hausbrauerei** at the Altstadthof on Bergstrasse 19. This is an old brewery reassembled and put back into production making an unfiltered dark beer which can be tasted on draft or purchased in bottles. We discovered it after closing time (7:00 pm) and cannot report on it since we left town before it opened the next day (2:00 pm).

Bayreuth is about an hour from Nürnberg and is well known as the center of Wagnerian culture. There is a Richard Wagner Museum and a *Festspielhaus,* a custom built theatre for Wagnerian music dramas. Bayreuth also has a brewery well-known to Americans; we decided to go there and thence to Hof, criss-crossing the Fränkische regions as we knew there should be many small breweries to find. **Privatbrauerei Gebr. Maisel** in Bayreuth gave us very little new to taste, its importer having done a very thorough job. There were a few as follows: **MAISEL'S KRISTALLKLAR WEIZEN** — deep bright gold, big head, tart nose, lactic acid and cloves start the flavor, softens as it goes, smooth light dry malt aftertaste, nicely balanced and very drinkable; **MAISEL HEFE WEISSE** — hazy amber, big head, light lactic-malt aroma, big clove flavor, zesty and bright, hefty body, refreshing and dry, dry malt finish and aftertaste; **MAISEL BRÄU SPEZIAL** — pale copper-gold, malt nose with an artificially sweet quality, palate similar but more noticeable, complex but strange and unbalanced, highly carbonated, pleasant malt and hop aftertaste has good length; and **MAISEL'S WEIZEN BOCK** — cloudy brown, has sediment, very foamy, fruity wheat grain and apple peel aroma, initially some lactic acid on the palate, but it didn't last, promises sweetness but stays dry, full but not heavy, high carbonation balances complex flavors rather than intrudes, long on the palate, feels good in your mouth, very good of type.

A brewery not far from Bayreuth is **Privatbrauerei Eschenbacher-Wagner Bräu** in Eschenbach. We found only one of their labels, but it was a good one: **ESCHENBACHER EDEL MÄRZEN,** a hazy amber brew with a roasted malt and dry hop aroma, complex palate exactly like the nose, excellent balance, very drinkable, full bodied and full flavored and very long and satisfying.

The town of Marktredwitz is also in the area and there we found **Privatbrauerei Kaiserhofbräu** in Märkstetter Marktredwitz. Their labels were **FRÄNKISCH WEIZEN HEFE DUNKEL** — amber-brown, faint spicy malt nose, off chemical taste of banana and phenolic, sweet malt aftertaste with odd components. Brewed under contract for

*Marco
Getränktmarkt
in Kulmbach.*

Marco Getränktmarkt of Kulmbach; **KAISERHOF FESTBIER** — deep gold, lactic hop and malt aroma, smoked malt flavor, dry smooth smoked malt aftertaste; and **KLOSTER-LANDBIER** — dark brown, roasted malt nose with a little smoke, even more smoke flavor is almost burnt, long lightly smoked malt aftertaste. **Brauerei Märkelsteiner** is also in Marktredwitz, offering **BRAUMEISTER HELL** — deep gold, hop nose, light off-dry malt flavor, hops in back, long malt aftertaste is a little more dry. The Marco Getränktmarkts are many and are well supplied with numbers of products from the area. They are an excellent source for some of those hard to find brews from the smaller local towns and may save you many miles and hours.

The Frankenwald region is small but is an extremely fertile hunting area for beer. In Hof, we knew of the large **Deininger Kronenbräu A.G.**, but found only beers readily available in the U.S. We had better luck with the smaller **Privatbrauerei Scherdel** and its **SCHERDEL PILSNER PREMIUM** — gold, complex malt and hop nose, big complex flavor like the aroma, spruce or pine in the finish, long dry malt aftertaste; and **Hofer Bierbrauerei** which makes **FRÄNKISCH FEST BIER** — deep gold, papery malt nose, big malt flavor, dull malt finish and aftertaste, a bit off-dry and somewhat flabby. Made for Marco Getränktmarkts of the Nürnberg-Kulmbach area. **Brauerei Gampert** in Weissenbrunn/Kronach makes **GAMPERTBRÄU FÖRSTER PILS** — gold, unusual complex malt and carbonation nose, hop and off-dry malt flavor, long dry malt aftertaste. Also in Weissenbrunn is **Brauhaus Weissenbrunn**, which has exported their Oktober Bier and Adler Bräu to the U.S. In Mitwitz, the **Franken Brauerei** produces **FRANKEN BRÄU PILSENER PREMIUM** — gold, big hop nose and flavor, plenty of malt in support, very big body, solid flavor, very well-balanced, big long malt and hop aftertaste; **FRANKEN BRÄU KELLER GOLD DUNKEL** — brown, rich roast malt aroma and flavor, no harshness, very smooth, good body and balance, long dry roasted malt aftertaste, a delicious brew; and **FRANKEN BRÄU FEST BIER** — gold, good hop and malt aroma, very appetizing nose, big flavor has hops but is mostly malt, very fine balance, rich tasting, good body, dry hop finish, long dry aftertaste has plenty of both hops and malt. Another is **Privat Landbrauerei Strössner** in Ahornberg, maker of **AHORNBERGER MAIBOCK** — bright gold, malt nose, big rich malt flavor, slightly bitter hop finish, long light malt aftertaste, very pleasant.

One of the cities in the area that is very famous for its beers is Kulmbach. In fact, Kulmbach is famous mostly because of its beer. EKU Kulminator 28 (the 28 is degrees Plato denoting an extremely high density) and Reichelbräu's Eisbock (at 24 degrees) are probably the most notable, uniquely made by freezing the beer to increase the density and alcohol. Among its breweries are **Kulmbacher Schweizerhofbrau**, whose bock was one of the best German beers ever sent abroad (and which is no longer exported), **Monchshof Brauerei Gmbh**, many of whose very fine beers are regularly found in the U.S., the **Sandlerbrauerei**, which has sent us **KULMBACHER SANDLER-BRÄU PILS**, a pale golden pils with a toasted malt aroma and mild hop flavor, **Reichelbrauerei Kulmbach**, which has been kind enough to send us many fine brews, but has not let us have the extraordinary **KULMBACHER REICHELBRÄU EISBOCK 24,** a deep brown brew with a rich complex off-dry aromatic malt nose, body so huge it seems thick, very rich heavy malt flavor like a smooth malt tonic, very complex malt flavors, high alcohol and a long concentrated malt aftertaste and **Erste Kulmbacher Actienbrauerei, A.G.**, which exports almost everything they make. Some of the scarcer items are: **EKU KULMINATOR DUNKLER DOPPELBOCK** — bright deep amber, complex sweet toasted malt and licorice nose, malt is like Ovaltine, big grainy malt flavor, very heavy and filling, but very good and very long; **EKU JUBILÄUMSBIER** — bright tawny-gold, appetizing malt and hop aroma that fills a room, marvelous malt and hop flavor starts out off-dry and finishes with bright hops, long dry hop aftertaste has a hint of roasted malt in back, good balance, wonderful festbier; **EKU KULMBACHER HELLER MAIBOCK** — bright deep gold, creamy head, off-dry malt and hop nose, huge body, complex malt and hop flavor that is generally dry except the finish is off-dry, long fairly dry hop aftertaste, very good balance; **EKU OKTOBERFEST** — bright gold, good hop and malt aroma, not big but pleasant, light complex malt and hop flavor, dry hop finish and aftertaste with a touch of sour malt at the end; and **EKU EDELBOCK** — deep gold, flowery fruity off-dry malt and hop aroma, very appetizing, palate is big off-dry malt in front and middle, finishes caramel sweet, hops appear in the aftertaste behind the caramel, but way behind, long full and rich malt aftertaste, a little light on the hops, but very delicious.

In nearby Weismain there is **Püls-Bräu** with **PÜLS-BRÄU KRONE PILS**, a golden beer with a big hop nose, zesty malt and hop flavor (as you sip it the hops gradually take a more and more prominent position on the palate), big body and a long dry hop aftertaste. In Altenkunstadt, we have **Brauerei Leikeim** and three more beers; **LEIKEIM DAS ORIGINAL** — gold, complex malt nose, tangy malt flavor is very hefty and well-backed with strong hops, big body, long aftertaste has plenty of both malt and hops, the malt dominates throughout this big flavored brew, yet there is harmony among the components, a lusty brew; **LEIKEIM WEISSE (MIT SEINER HEFE)** — hazy gold, huge thick head, fruity-spicy malt nose, smooth creamy fruity-spicy malt flavor, dry malt aftertaste, good body and balance, very drinkable; and **ALT KUNESTATER URSTOFF** — amber-brown, malt nose, big dry roasted malt flavor, good body, long off-dry malt aftertaste.

Our goal for this day was to reach Lichtenfels. There we knew of another Privater Brauereigasthof, **Privatbrauerei Gasthof Wichert** which provided us **WICHERT PILSENER** — gold, aromatic hop nose, hop and malt flavor, dry hop finish, long dry hop aftertaste and **WICHERT DUNKLES** — brown, malt aroma, lightly smoked malt flavor, long and dry malt aftertaste, a pleasant good tasting brew. There were no rooms available, so we went on to nearby Ebelsbach and Hotel Klosterbräu Ebelsbach. All 15 rooms were available and we were able to enjoy their two labels **EBELSBACHER KLOSTERBRÄU KLOSTER-HELL** — deep gold, hop nose, plenty of malt support, big malt flavor, dry malt and hop aftertaste and **EBELSBACHER KLOSTERBRÄU KLOSTER-PILS** — deep gold, hop nose, good hop and malt flavor, a bright taste, good body and balance, long dry hop and malt aftertaste, a likeable brew and easy to drink. Unfortunately, we landed there on the one day of the week the restaurant was closed, so we had to go elsewhere for supper and were able to taste the beer only in bottle, instead of on draft.

We dined in Eltmann, only about 2 km distant and found that it is the home of the excellent beers of **Privatbrauerei Wagner/Weiss Rössl Bräu**. The extensive list of these brews includes **WEISS RÖSSL LEONARDI BOCK** — brown, lovely lightly toasted malt nose, big malt flavor, excellent balance, good body, good tasting long malt after-taste; **WEISS RÖSSL RATSHERREN DUNKEL** — brown, cereal malt aroma and flavor, good body, long dry malt aftertaste; **WEISS RÖSSL FESTBIER** — deep gold, pleasant malt aroma, good dry malt flavor, medium long very dry malt aftertaste, good hop balance; **WEISS RÖSSL MÄRZEN** — deep gold, toasted malt nose, very nice, lovely toasted malt flavor finishes richly, smooth dry medium long malt aftertaste; **WEISS RÖSSL FRANKEN RAUCHBIER** — deep amber, aroma like smoked bacon, smoked salty meat flavor, fades a bit at the finish but remains on the palate for a very long time; **WEISS RÖSSL URSTOFF** — pale gold, complex malt aroma, pleasant straightforward malt flavor, light body, pleasant and very drinkable, medium long dry malt aftertaste; and **KARLSKRONE** — gold, hop and toasted malt aroma, flavor to match, sour hop finish and long dry sour hop aftertaste. This beer is made for ALDI, Mulheim A.D., Ruhr. Another brewery near Eltmann is **Brauerei Krug** in Ebelsbach/Main. They have **KRUG EDEL HELL** — gold, sour hop nose and taste, good body, long aftertaste like the flavor; **KRUG GOLDEN PILS** — gold, malt and hop nose, hop and malt flavor, good balance, dry hop finish is softened by a good level of malt, long dry hop and malt aftertaste; **KRUG ALT FRÄNKISCH** — deep amber, roasted malt nose and taste, creamy, dry but rich, slightly toasted dry malt finish, long dry malt aftertaste; **KRUG HEILIG LÄNDER** — golden amber, big malt nose and taste, malt finish, dry malt aftertaste, seems to be some faint hops in the aftertaste, but largely this is a malt only beer; and **KRUG WEISSE** — hazy gold, big spicy lactic nose, light spicy flavor, creamy, dry malt aftertaste has some length.

Also in that area we found **Privatbrauerei Ambros Brütting** in Staffelstein with **HOFLIEFERANT EXPORT EXQUISIT** — tawny-gold, big toasted malt nose and flavor, dry malt finish, long dry malt and hop aftertaste, good body and good balance; **HOFLIEFERANT BAYRISCH HELL** — gold, malt nose, high carbonation, flavor has only light malt and hops, dull malt finish, faint hops join the malt in the brief aftertaste; and **HOFLIEFERANT BOCK BIER** — amber-gold, big rich hop and toasted malt nose, huge rich roasted malt flavor, long rich aftertaste is a continuation of the flavor, high alcohol (7%) is not noticeable in the rich malt flavor, a finely balanced excellent bock.

Bamberg:
How Good (or bad) is
Smoked Beer at the Source?

Our experience with Bamberger smoked beer was largely with the **Kaiserdom Rauchbier** imported by Merchant du Vin. As our first *rauchbier* (smoked beer), it was interesting, but it seemed the smokiness was somewhat overdone. Was it extra smoky for the export market? Was this the way the Bambergers liked it? We were determined to find out as we headed into the town, but wait. What was that bar we just passed? It looked suspiciously like a brew-pub. We did a U-turn and headed back and found the **Brauerei Bayer**, a brew-pub in Viereth. Inside the pub, they were sticking a hot poker into the beer before serving it. I had heard of this practice, but saw it here for the first and only time. The beer was **BAYER MÄRZEN** — deep amber-brown, strong malt nose with a fruity character, big fruity-malt flavor, long aftertaste like the flavor. It would be better if drier, as the fruit is sort of candy-like. Perhaps it is made that way to balance off the smoky effects of the poker heated in wood coals.

Back on track to Bamberg, we were familiar with the beers of **Privatbrauerei Burgerbräu Wörner OHG** and the Kaiserdom line, including the aforementioned Rauchbier. Most Kaiserdom beers are readily available in the U.S. with the exception of **KAISERDOM UR-BOCK STARKBIER** — medium deep amber, mellow toasted malt nose, soft and smooth toasted malt palate, good intensity, no faults, long aftertaste like the flavor, and **KAISERDOM HEFE WEISSBIER** — hazy amber, faint clove and wheat aroma, refreshing spicy clove, yeast

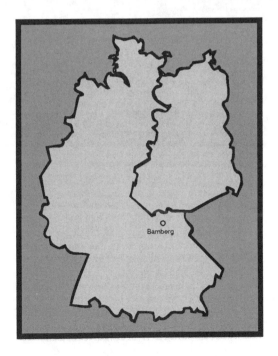

and wheat flavor, light and smooth, pleasant finish, medium long clean, dry aftertaste like the flavor. Another brewery found in Bamberg was **Privatbrauerei Löwenbräu Bamberg K.G.**, which brews **ST. STEPHANUS FEST BIER** — amber, fruity malt aroma, pleasant malt and hop flavor, fairly dry, good balance, medium body, brief length; **BAMBERGER LÖWENBRÄU FRÄNKISCHES URBIER** — deep amber, sweet clean malt nose, off-dry malt and hop flavor, plenty of alcohol, medium body, long malt aftertaste stays off-dry; and **BAMBERGER LÖWENBRÄU EXPORT** — deep gold, rich malt nose and flavor, complex and tasty, good body, long dry malt aftertaste, very good with food or by itself, one of Germany's best export style beers. One of the many small breweries in the city is **Privatbrauerei Kaiserbräu**, brewer of **BAMBERGER KRONEN PREMIUM PILSENER BEER** — bright gold, beautiful hop nose, strong hop flavor, long dry hop aftertaste borders on being bitter.

We were concerned about finding some of the very small breweries because the information we had regarding their whereabouts was scanty at best. We travelled much of the historic city by foot and the rest slowly by auto, searching every street for these well hidden establishments. We found all but one of those whose names we had and one which we had not been told about.

Privater Brauereigasthof Greifenklau.

There was **Brauerei Spezial**, one of Bamberg's Brauereigasthofs (Obere König Str.) They have only 7 rooms, a fine restaurant, and **SPEZIAL RAUCHBIER LAGER** — amber, meaty smoked malt nose, very dry smoked malt flavor, dry malt finish and aftertaste has the smoke but it gradually sets in far to the back, and **SPEZIAL RAUCHBIER MÄRZEN** — deep amber, meaty smoked malt aroma, big flavor like the nose, smooth, very tasty and very drinkable, there's a hidden sweetness in there also, complex and interesting, medium dry long malt aftertaste with a faint smoky background. Now, I see why the Bambergers like rauch bier. It is well in back, and it does not get in the way of the beer flavor. Very nicely done with a light hand.

We stepped onto the sidewalk and across the street was a brew-pub, the **Privatbrauerei Fässla**. The Fässla also had very good food and **FÄSSLA GOLD PILS** — gold, very nice appetizing hop nose, plenty of malt in back, big malt and hop flavor, dry and delicious, big bodied, long dry hop aftertaste still has plenty of malt in support for good balance, good brew; **FÄSSLA HELL LAGER BIER** — pale amber, light malt nose and flavor, medium body, medium long dry hop aftertaste; and **ECHTES BAMBERGER ZWERGLA** — brown, roasted malt nose, strong heavily roasted malt flavor, good body, extremely long roasted malt aftertaste (strongest flavored aftertaste I've experienced), fairly pleasant despite its almost overwhelming strength across the palate. No smoked beer here, but interesting brews nevertheless, and an unexpected find. The **Privater Brauereigasthof Greifenklau** (Laurenzinplatz) has 42 rooms, a restaurant and a large parking lot (a consideration in Bamberg). They also have a very good smoked beer: **GREIFENKLAU EXPORT** — amber-gold, good appetizing malt and hop aroma, delicately smoked malt flavor, long dry slightly smoked malt aftertaste, nicely done and very likeable. We also found **Brauerei Heller**, the **Schlenkerla Tavern** (Dominaker Str.) and **AECHT SCHLENKERLA RAUCHBIER MÄRZEN** — brown, appetizing smoked malt nose, not a meaty type smoke but more like the delicate smoking used with salmon, light fresh smoked flavor, hop finish, dry malt aftertaste has the smoke in behind, very nicely done. There is another Brauerei Gasthof in Bamberg, **Brauerei Keesmann**, but we could not locate it, even though we had the address (5 Wunderburg Str.).

Most of the beers found in Bamberg were from the city itself. They do have good beer and maybe the locals care little for beers from a distance. One exception was **Privatbrauerei Modscheidler KG** from nearby Buttenheim with its striking **ST. GEORGEN BRÄU DUNKELER DOPPELBOCK** — brown, excellent dry malt nose with good hops in support, big malt flavor again with plenty of hop backing, big body, complex, long dry malt aftertaste with the hops dropping out early.

The town of Bamberg itself is most attractive. Since we covered most of it on foot, we got to see quite a bit of it. Bamberg is built on seven hills, which means you do a lot of climbing up and down on twisting narrow streets, and each hill and hollow seems to have its own character, pehaps because they were populated at different periods. On the crown of the main hill sits the Domstadt (a huge church and related buildings) over-looking the Regnitz and the lower city across that river where one finds the downtown business district. The small city is very Baroque, and most interesting. Next time I will spend more time in Bamberg. The city and the beers were very interesting, but our time was running out and we had to visit Würzburg which we knew only from being a center for the Franken wines and the home of **Würzburger Hofbrau, A.G.,** one of the breweries that has continued to send us a variety of excellent beers, including seasonal specialties, like the May Bock, Holiday beer, and Oktoberfest.

Privatbrauerei Fässla in Bamberg.

Wonderful Würzburg

The hotels of certain cities tend to be expensive compared to those of small country towns which are never very far away. Problems of high tariff and crowded parking lots can be solved simply by heading out of town for 10 km or so and finding a gasthaus in some small village. That is how the Hotel Gasthof *Zum Weissen Ross* was chosen in the very small town of Gossmannsdorf, a very short distance from Ochsenfurt. That is also how to discover the beers of **Brauerei D. Oechsner** of Ochsenfurt.

The restaurant at the *Zum Weissen Ross* (white horse) offered inviting aromas and, being basically weak when it comes to good food, it seemed a good choice for dinner. I tried a beer from **Br. Kauzen** (also located in Ochsenfurt) while Bill tried the Oechsner Pils. One sip and he held out the glass for me to try. "Jim, you have got to taste this." I did and exclaimed "My God, it's a perfect pilsener." It was, and so were the next two or three. We also tasted the Märzen and found it not to be wanting. The next night we ate in Ochsenfurt and found the Heller Bock. We also finished off their supply. My notes say it all:

OECHSNER PREMIUM PILS — deep gold, delightful hop nose, zesty malt and hop flavor, mostly hops but with great supporting malt, good body, excellent balance, rich and smooth, very refreshing, long dry hop aftertaste retains the malt as well, this is a perfect Pilsener.

OECHSNER MÄRZEN EXPORT — gold, big bright hop and malt aroma, very tasty rich hop and malt flavor, feels great in your mouth, good body, rich and very long hop and malt aftertaste, an absolute treasure and perhaps the best Märzen in my experience.

OECHSNER HELLER BOCK — deep gold, extremely complex huge hop aroma, intense hop and malt flavor, expertly balanced, a lip-smacking big complex brew that offers an abundance of everything but

o Würzburg

doesn't assault the palate, incredible brew, extremely long fine aftertaste much like the flavor.

I said before that Ochsenfurt has another brewery. It is **Brauerei Kauzen**, maker of weissbier. We found two brews from this brewery that has a *kauz* (a small owl) for its logo: **KAUZEN DUNKELER KAUZ DUNKLES HEFE WEISSBIER** — deep hazy amber, big head, rich wheat-malt nose, very complex with tobacco and chocolate, carbonation, grains, sour malt, faint spices, good while it lasts but it cuts off quickly once swallowed; and **KAUZEN HEFE-WEISSBIER** — cloudy gold, lightly spiced soapy malt nose, pleasantly spiced malt flavor, medium body, somewhat dull dry malt aftertaste.

Würzburg is a beautiful small university city situated on the Main River which gently flows between rolling hills, some of which tower over the city. Because Würzburg was a seat of learning with little or no war industry, most thought it would not be bombed. They were wrong. In 1945, it was the victim of a serious air strike, part of the allies' plan to make sure that no citizen of a German city should fail to experience an air raid. While many of the damaged buildings were never restored (as was done in other cities like Nürnberg), there is still much to see and enjoy. There is the Marienberg Fortress towering over the city on the left bank of the Main, the Residenz palace with its magnificent architecture and art, and the Marienkapelle, a lovely 14th century Gothic church. Of course, I could be happy just eating the fine Franconian cuisine while enjoying the local wines and beer. The wines are greatly underrated on our shores and the local beer is as good as any you can find in the world.

The only house brewery in town is the **Erste Würzburger Hausbrauerei** on Burkarder Str. serving unfiltered beer and Franconian dishes. There are many fine small breweries in nearby towns, many with their beers on tap on the premises. Four brews were found from **Privatbrauerei Ehnle** of Lauterbach. **LAUTERBACHER HEFEWEIZEN** had an unusual spicy-pine character that was pleasant but short. **LAUTERBACH SCHLANKE WEISSE** was pleasantly spicy, but very light, not unexpectedly since it is a low alcohol brew. **LAUTERBACH URHELL** had an off-dry malt nose, dry malt palate and aftertaste. It was alright, but no raves. The big winner in Lauterbach and a surprise, considering the ordinary nature of their other beers, was **LAUTERBACH BROTZEITBIER** with its huge hop and roasted malt aroma, delicious flavor that matched the nose, great balance, and great length. It was one of the best tasting and most drinkable beers we found on our tour.

Another brewery in the Würzburg area is **Privatbrauerei Kesselring** in Marksteft am Main. Their beers were **MARUHN PILS** — bright gold, good hop aroma, medium dry hopped malt flavor, highly carbonated. slight papery mid-palate, dry finish and short dry hop aftertaste. Made for B. Maruhn of Der Grosste Biermarkt der Welt of Pfungstadt; **UR FRÄNKISCHES LANDBIER** — amber, toasted malt nose, malt palate, no complexity, malt finish, short malt aftertaste; **KESSELRING PILS** — gold, bright hop nose with malt in back, very bright flavor like the nose, malt rolls in at mid-palate and stays into the long rich malt aftertaste, good body, bright zesty brew, one of the better Pilseners encountered; and **SCHLEMMER WEISSBIER MIT HEFE** — hazy gold, dry malt nose, faintly spicy malt flavor, long dry malt aftertaste has no spicy component, very drinkable and refreshing.

From **Burgerliches Brauhaus Spessart** in Wiesen there was **WIESENER RÄUBER BOCK** — amber, big very rich malt nose, huge malt flavor, big body, rich, strong, smooth and very long. And from **Werner-Bräu**, a brewery in Poppenhausen, there was **WERNER PILSENER** — gold, malt and hop aroma and flavor, quite tasty, excellent balance, long dry hop and malt aftertaste. **Brauerei Stumpf** in Lohr, which has exported a number of beers over the past decade or so, came up with **KEILER WEISSBIER DUNKEL** — amber, light wheat beer nose (some malt, some wheat, some cloves), light spicy clove flavor, very mild, highly carbonated, light body, fairly long aftertaste like the flavor. From **Schlossbrauerei Soldenau** in Soldenau we tasted **ORIGI-**

Privater Brauereigasthof Düll.

NAL ALT BAYERISCHE UR WEISSE — deep amber, big head, big aroma of malt with faint lactic-clove spice way in back, light piquant clove flavor, some soapiness in the finish, light body, dull soapy malt aftertaste. Bottled for Privatbrauerei Will, Motten. Also from Soldenau was **SOLDENAUER SCHLOSS DUNKLES WEISSBIER** — very slightly hazy amber, aroma is mostly malt but there is some faint spicy cloves in back, flavor is largely malt with some sourness in mid-palate, and a dry malt finish and aftertaste, the lactic stays in back but doesn't leave, an interesting brew.

On Sunday morning, as we were about to depart the area, we wandered out into the countryside near Ochsenfurt to find Gnodstadt and yet another brewery guest house. **Privater Brauereigasthof Düll** was not yet open, but the cleaning girl was hard at work and sold us a bottle each of their beers, but only because we had empty *fläschen* (bottles) to return. **DÜLL BOCK** was golden amber, had a very complex malt and hop nose, wonderfully appetizing big strong malt flavor, big hops as well, high alcohol (6.8%), and a long and strong aftertaste like the flavor. **DÜLL PILS** was bright gold, had a malt nose, malt flavor that starts off-dry, but finishes dry leading into a dry malt aftertaste with some hop sourness at the very end. **DÜLL MÄRZEN** was gold, had a malt nose, dry malt flavor, and a long dry malt aftertaste has some tones of vegetable, herbs and honey.

So what of **Würzburger Hofbrau, A.G.?** I am happy to tell that we have access in the U.S. to all of their products that I saw in Germany, except that there you can taste them on tap.

The Odenwald

We headed due west from Würzburg on small back roads through the Odenwald. Eventually we planned to reach Heidelberg after searching the region for new beers. It is an area generally ignored by books on beer as they tend to focus on the more famous locations, but we knew there were many fine small breweries. Since there are no towns of any appreciable size in the Odenwald, we had to "cruise" the region.

One of the first breweries we came across was **J. Wörner & Sohne KG Erbacher Brauhaus** in Erbach. They provided us with one of the delights of the trip, **ERBACHER PRÄDIKATOR DOPPELBOCK** — deep amber-brown, delightful rich sweet malt nose, big rich malt with an earthy background, medium dry long malt; a delicious brew.

Next was **Schwannen-Brauerei A.G. & Co., K.G.** in Schwetzingen with **SCHÖFFERHOFER WEIZEN** — pale yellow-gold, dusty clove and malt aroma, sweet malt and clove flavor, good body, spicy malt finish and aftertaste drier than the flavor; and **SCHÖFFERHOFER HEFEWEIZEN** — hazy gold, bright spicy hop nose, zesty spicy hop and malt flavor, creamy and smooth, long dry spicy malt aftertaste.

In Beerfelden (there would have to be a brewery there), **Privatbrauerei Felsenkeller** makes **MÜMLINGTHALER SCHANKBIER** — pale bright gold, dank fruity nose, dry fruity malt taste, some sourness in the finish, long dry aftertaste (schankbier is low alcohol beer) and **BEERFELDER FELSENBOCK** — amber, light malt nose has a chemical-like component, malt flavor is tasty but lacks zest, medium body, medium length malt aftertaste.

Privatbrauerei Schmucker in Mossautal provided another winner: **SCHMUCKER DOPPEL-BOCK DUNKEL** — deep amber-brown, rich dry malt nose, perfect balance, delicious dry roast malt palate, very long with great depth of flavor, excellent double bock.

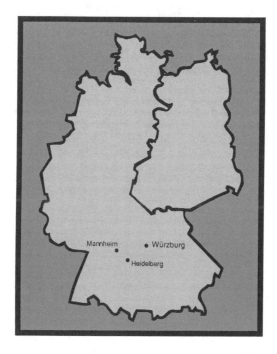

L. Schönberger Sohne from Gross-Bieberau offers some winning tastes with **SCHÖNBERGER FEST BOCK** — deep amber-brown, big roasted malt aroma, complex rich malt flavor up front on the palate, pungent hops in back that show best in the finish, good balance, medium to long malt and hop aftertaste, a marvelous tasting brew; **SCHÖNBERGER UR-BOCK** — copper-amber, huge roasted malt aroma and flavor, flavor is drier than the nose and has many subtle nuances, long complex malt aftertaste, 6% alcohol, excellent brew; and **SCHÖNBERGER ODENWALDER LANDBIER** — gold, hop nose, palate has more malt than hops but the balance is very good, good body, long dry malt aftertaste has hops showing well at the very end. All their beers are worth finding.

We arrived in Heidelberg near lunch time and decided on the Europäschehof, the big fancy hotel in the center of Heidelberg. Every now and then you have to splurge, and this is a good place to do it. Waiters in formal dress, walls with inlaid wood, flowers, and beautifully appointed throughout; it sets the mood for genteel dining. Also they had two beers from **Heidelberger Schlossquell Brauerei, A.G.** The **VALENTINS KLARES WEIZENBIER** was bright gold with a big dense head, clean grainy malt aroma with a touch of refreshing clove-lactic spice, clean fresh bright flavor is like the nose but better, and a lingering wheat and malt aftertaste. It is delicious, refreshing, and very drinkable. **HEIDELBERGER SCHLOSSQUELL PILS** was gold, had a complex hop and malt nose, zesty hop and malt flavor and a long, dry hop aftertaste.

Well lunched and fully beered, we stepped out in brilliant sunshine and a warmer than usual afternoon in Heidelberg. Although it was a bit early in the year for foreign tourists that mob the town in the summer, a warm Sunday in May makes it a favorite place for the locals to see their town, especially the Schloss, one of the world's great castles. When I first visited the Schloss in 1967, you could drive up the hill to it, park in the yard and wander through it at will. There was nothing there to disturb, the contents having been sacked hundreds of years ago when the structure was largely destroyed in the 17th century. Now, the biggest problem is where to park your vehicle so you can climb the hill to the site. It is worth the climb (there is a bus also), but we beer drinkers have to work it off. There is a fine view of the city from the Schloss. In fact, picture postcard views of Heidelberg abound. Almost any open spot from ground level on up will bring your camera to your eye for a snap. We climbed the hill and took the tour of the castle, now well organized for tourists.

By reputation, Heidelberg is expensive, but I have always managed to find modestly priced digs, although modest here is a bit more pricey than modest in most other German cities. A good thing to know is that for about $1, the tourist office will find you a room, a buck well spent if you are there at the height of the tourist season.

Heidelberg is also home to an exciting array of dining and entertainment establishments. Hauptstrasse and its side streets can offer you anything you can imagine and more. The famous student taverns should not be missed. Some of the most famous for beer are the Roter Ochsen, Zum Sepp'l, and Schnookeloch. For restaurants there is Perkeo, the Schlossquell-Bräustubl, and a house-brewery called Vetters Alt-Heidelberger Brauhaus. If you are pub crawling, start with the Biermuseum which boasts over 100 brews, ten or so on draft. You may not have to go further.

Also from the area we found **Brauerei K. Silbernagel A.G** .from Bellheim and its **BELLHEIMERSILBER BOCK** — gold, sweet malt and hop nose, malt palate with light hops, strong but not powerful, long medium dry malt aftertaste, stays very drinkable.

Between Heidelberg and Frankfurt, one of the most commonly seen names is Eichbaum. **Eichbaum Brauerei, AG.** in Mannheim produces a wide range of very good brews including: **EICHBAUM FESTBIER** — pale amber, faint malt and hop nose, faintly sweet malt palate, some hops arrive for the finish, slightly sour and bitter long hop aftertaste; **EICHBAUM APOSTULATOR** — brilliant pale ruby-brown, big toasted malt nose has a brief puff of cherry at the beginning, big complex fruity malt flavor, long malt aftertaste seems a bit smoky, a real lip smacking brew; **EICHBAUM EXPORT ALTGOLD** — bright gold, good malt and hop aroma and flavor, fine balance, smooth and mellow, medium body, medium long aftertaste like the flavor; **EICHBAUM PILSENER EICHKRONE** — bright pale gold, good well-hopped aroma, bright hop flavor, long complex aftertaste with both hops and malt; **EICHBAUM MAIBOCK** — pale amber-gold, big toasted malt aroma, sense of alcohol as well (6.6%), rich malt flavor, great balance with the hops, good body, long off-dry malt and hop aftertaste; **EICHBAUM KRISTALL WEIZEN** — bright gold, spicy lactic nose, fresh clove taste, clean and refreshing, medium length, a bit on the weak side; **EICHBAUM HEFE WEIZEN** — cloudy yellow-gold, slightly yeasty and spicy nose, complex flavor has some of the yeast, fairly smooth, definitely mellow, good carbonation level to give it balance, fairly long; and **EICHBAUM DUNKLES WEIZEN** — hazy amber, light lactic-spice nose, light malt and spice flavor, light body, pleasant and drinkable, finishes quite well and has a long malt and clove aftertaste.

Another Mannheim brewery is **Burgerliches Brauhaus Zum Habereckl PBH** with HABERECKL MÄRZEN — hazy amber, big head, off-sweet faintly acidic fading nose, crisp malt flavor with no acidity, some yeast in the finish, short malt aftertaste and the exciting **HABERECKL FEUERIO TROPFEN JAHRGANG STARKBIER** — deep ruby-brown, rich malt aroma, huge (no, enormous) rich malt flavor that lasts and lasts and lasts, one of the best examples found to prove what can be done with malt alone. This beer comes out each year with the date of issue on the label. I don't doubt that it can be cellared.

Westward To The Pfälzer Bergland

The Pfälz does have hilly country, but there are no very tall mountains and there are a lot of rolling hills covered with vineyards. It is a pretty countryside though not dramatic. I was well familiar with this region having lived here for a spell back over 30 years ago. Many former military people in the U.S. have fond memories and a taste for the beers of this region.

We drove through Landstuhl but did not stay there because my favorite restaurant was no longer in business and the town looked too much like an American base town. Instead we went on to Zweibrücken and put up at the Rosen Hotel, location of my first overnight stay in Germany some 30+ years ago. None of the restaurants I knew from that time have survived, but the Hotel Hitschler, right around the corner at Fruchtmarktstrasse 8, was recommended as being the restaurant having gained the best reputation in the town, and the meal was quite good.

One of the best of the local beer producers is **Parkbrauerei A.G.** with breweries in Pirmasens and Zweibrücken. Their line consists of : **PARKBRÄU EXPORT** — pale gold, light but very good hop aroma well-backed with malt, good body, creamy texture, bright tangy hop flavor and long dry hop aftertaste, good tasting refreshing brew; **PARKBRÄU PILS** — medium gold, zesty hop and lightly toasted malt nose, well-balanced lively hop and toasted malt flavor, good body, lightly bitter dry hop finish and aftertaste, straightforward well-made brew; and the excellent **PARKBRÄU PIRMINATOR** — deep bright gold, toasted malt nose, big bright rich malt flavor, high alcohol, big body, huge but very well-balanced, long dry hop aftertaste has plenty of

malt backing. In nearby Homburg is **Brauerei Karlsberg** and **KARLSBRÄU PILSENER** — deep golden amber, faint hop and malt aroma, flavor of yeast and malt, mild hop background, sour hop finish and aftertaste; **KARLSBRÄU MANNLICH** — bright yellow-gold, nice hop nose, good balance, off-dry malt and hop palate, hop finish, medium long dry hop aftertaste, good tasting satisfying brew; and **KARLSBERG BOCK** — deep rose-amber, faint malt aroma, light to medium body, light dry malt flavor, pleasant long dry malt aftertaste. The **Saarfurst Brewery** in Merzig, a subsidiary of Karlsberg, is reported to make a *Bier Eiche* (oak beer), but I have never found it. Also nearby is Kaiserslautern with **Bayerische Brauerei, A.G.**, more familiarly known as BBK. **BBK PILS** is pale bright gold, has a light hop nose, palate is mostly hops but there is some malt, fair balance but rather short and dull.

A number of items popped up here and there from small area brewers. There was **Brauerei Ottweiler** in Ottweil with **KARLSKRONE EDEL PILS** — gold, hop nose, dull malt flavor, long dry malt aftertaste. **Dillinger Brauhaus, Gmbh.** in Dillingen had **CONVIKT MEISTER-SCHUTZ** — gold, light malt nose, malt flavor, medium to short dry malt aftertaste, nice malt brew but lacks zest. **Brauerei Fuch** in Windesheim has **FUCH'S FEST BOCK** — amber, toasted malt nose, palate to match, medium body, very long toasted malt aftertaste, good balance between the malt and the hops. **Brauerei Hausmann** in Ramstein offers the impressive **RAMSTEINER EXCLUSIV PREMIUM PILSENER** — gold, some particulate matter in suspension, lovely light flowery aromatic hop nose, big hop flavor, plenty of body, lots of malt in back, slightly oxidized, long dry hop aftertaste, very drinkable and very good with food; and **RAMSTEINER EXCLUSIV PREMIUM DUNKEL** — amber, big toasted malt aroma, malty flavor is off-dry in front, dry by the finish, good body, loads of flavor, long dry malt aftertaste, has a rich quality, feels good in your mouth. Last, there was **Privatbrauerei Becker** in St. Ingbert (if you are looking on a German map for a town named Saint, the word is *Sankt*) which makes **BECKER'S JUBILÄUMSBOCK** — deep brown, big malt nose and taste, nice balance, has a chocolate character, fairly complex, good body, very long malt aftertaste, nice drinkable brew. Of course, here in the Rheinpfalz you are in **Bitburger** country where the beer of **Bitburger Brauerei Thomas Simon** is widely distributed. While I consider Bit to be too light and somewhat on the ordinary side, it is very bright and refreshing on draft. Another beer found in this area that is familiar to Americans is **Wicküler Pils** from **Privatbrauerei Franz Josef Wicküler** of Wuppertal. This is an excellent pils, not as dry and as well hopped as the northern German beers (which brewers in this region tend to favor), but rather a good compromise between that dry style and the fuller, maltier pils to the south.

One of the highlights of any trip to Germany is the town of Trier. It is the oldest city in Germany, founded by the Romans over 2000 years ago. It is a beautiful well-kept city with magnificent churches (the Dom and Liebfrauenkirche-which themselves date back 1600 years), Roman monuments and baths including the Konstantinbasilika and Porta Nigra, and many fine museums and libraries. It also has a fine brewery: **Löwenbräu Trier J. Mendgen** with **PETRISBERGER PILSENER FEINER ART** — pale yellow-gold, light hop nose, bright hop flavor, long dry hop aftertaste, some sour hops at the very end that linger on for quite a time; **TRIERER LÖWENBRÄU EDELPILS** — gold, light malt aroma, light hop and malt flavor, hop finish, long dry hop aftertaste;

TRIERER LÖWENBRÄU KURFURST EXPORT — pale gold, malt nose, malt front palate, dry hop finish, long hop aftertaste, very drinkable; and **TREUERER ALT** — brown, malt nose and big malt flavor, a bit sweet up front, drier at the middle and finish, long dry malt aftertaste.

From Trier, the road to Koblenz winds through the vineyards lining the banks of the Mosel River. This is amazing and beautiful wine country, with offerings of wine tastings every few hundred feet. There is beer, but nothing local, and it takes the distant back seat to the wines. Village after village pass behind us. Piesport, Bernkastel, Zell, and other names famous to wine lovers. Near Koblenz we cut over to the Rhein and began passing more famous names like Rudesheim, Bingen, Assmanhausen, and Eltville. Alas, there was too little time. Our flight home was but two days ahead. We had to "do" the Frankfurt area before leaving Germany. The wine pilgrimage would have to wait for another trip. New beer was scarce in this area. Only **St. Martin Brauerei Fohr OHG** in Lahnstein/Rhein showed up with **SCHNEE BOCK** — deep amber, both hops and malt in nose, strong malt and hop flavor, good balance, plenty of alcohol as well (7.5%), long malt aftertaste, good tasting bock; and **LAHNSTEINER JÄGER-BOCK** — amber, very complex nose with hops, banana fruit and malt, strong malt flavor, very intense, big body, lots of alcohol (you can feel it in your mouth, nose, and sinuses), very long strong malt aftertaste, a blockbuster bock.

The Last Leg

With Frankfurt being a likely point of departure from Germany, some comment is appropriate. It is a big busy city and, like most big busy cities, it can offer a wide range of entertainment from a great zoo to great night life. It was largely destroyed in two massive air raids in 1944, and much of it was replaced with modern buildings. There is the restored Römerberg medieval quarter, beautiful churches and cathedrals, cloisters, museums and art galleries. For dining and drinking, you may wish to try Frankfurt's *Apfelwein*, an alcoholic cider that is available in four types. There is *Süsser* (sweet), *Heller* (light/pale), *Alte* (old and cloudy), and *Rauscher* (strong/bold). For beer, there is **Zwölf Apostel,** a house brewery on Rosenberger Strasse that supposedly serves organically brewed pils. I have also heard of similar establishments at nearby Eltville and Sachsenhausen. The one in Eltville is owned by Otto Binding and is called the **Kleines Eltviller Brauhaus.**

Over the years, I found that Neu-Isenberg and vicinity was a good place to spend one's last night in Germany. The town is equipped with good shopping areas, including a large modern mall. In addition to several restaurants that have given much pleasure over the past twenty years, the town also has three restaurants very highly rated by Michelen. We planned two dinners and one lunch in the town so that we might hit at least the three highly rated ones. For a good meal at a reasonable price, you may try Deutsche Haus on Bahnhof Strasse (a few blocks up from the *bahnhof*, or train station), with its Balkan specialties. Be sure to get guidance from your waiter (who does speak English) because those Balkan dishes will likely present words that are not in your German-English dictionary. A good place just off the main drag (Frankfurt Str.) is the Grunen Baum (Green Tree) with traditional German fare and a pleasant courtyard dining area (if the weather is good). One of the highly

rated restaurants is the Am Kamin at Frankfurt Str. 1. They had an outstanding veal ragout and deserve more investigation. This may be the finest restaurant in town. We also planned saturation beer tasting of the local brews, going out, as it were, in a blaze of glory.

The big breweries of Frankfurt are Binding and Henninger. **Binding Brauerei, A.G.** is best known to Americans for Clausthaler (one of the better non-alcoholic brews exported from Germany), but make some big time brews with alcohol. Locally they make **RÖMER PILS** — yellow-gold, sweet hop nose, brief off-dry malt flavor, light body, light medium dry malt aftertaste with hops in back; and **CAROLUS DER STARKE DOPPELBOCK** — very deep ruby-brown color, big rich sweet malt aroma with an unusual fruit-like component, big body, huge powerful dry malt flavor, complex, high alcohol, medium long dry malt aftertaste, very drinkable brew. **Henninger Brauerei KGuA** produces many beers that are exported under the same or slightly different names. For their local markets thay make **HENNINGER KAISER PILSENER** — deep gold, appetizing hop aroma, excellent malt and hop flavor, extremely dry, pleasant dry finish and long dry hop aftertaste, finely balanced, bright and refreshing; **HENNINGER KAISER EXPORT** — tawny-gold, balanced hop and malt nose and taste, hops in front, malt middle, hop finish and aftertaste; **KARAMALZ ALKOHOLFREIES MALZGETRÄNK** — deep red, light smoky-sweet malt nose, slightly smoky sweet malt flavor, long sweet malt aftertaste; **HENNINGER HELLER BOCK** — gold, lovely malt and hop aroma, big balanced malt and hop flavor, a tasty lip-smacking brew, very smooth, long malt aftertaste, beautifully made; **HENNINGER DOPPELBOCK** — deep brown, big dry roasted malt aroma, very complex, huge flavor is dry rich malt, finishes big with off-dry malt, long dry malt aftertaste, so much flavor you don't even notice the 8.1% alcohol, an almost perfect double bock; and **HENNINGER DUNKEL** — deep brown, rich malt nose and taste, dry malt finish and long dry malt aftertaste, excellent balance, very well-made beer.

Other breweries in the area that contribute to the local market are: **Marburger Brauerei Otto Beyer** in Marburg with **ALT MAR-BURGER DUNKEL** — brilliant amber, dry malt nose and flavor, aftertaste is a continuation of the flavor as well and is only medium in duration, there is a touch of sourness at the very end, so-so beer, but it does grow on you if you keep drinking it; **Heylands Brauerei Gmbh.** in Aschaffenburg with **HEYLANDS FESTBOCK** — brilliant deep gold, lovely sweet creamy roasted malt nose and taste, richness is maintained throughout, off-dry front, dry middle, sweet finish, long dry malt aftertaste, finely carbonated, a beautifully made delicious brew, **SEPPLS URBRÄU PREMIUM DUNKEL** — medium deep amber, complex rich malt aroma, light malt flavor, medium body, medium long light dry malt aftertaste, **HEYLANDS SEPPL-BOCK DUNKEL** — brown, dry toasted malt nose, flavor to match, very smooth, long dry malt aftertaste, richly flavored, and the 7% alcohol is barely noticeable amid all that malt, and **SEPPLS URBRÄU DUNKEL** — medium deep brown, good toasted malt nose, dry malt flavor, medium body, faintly sour dry malt aftertaste; **Jhring-Melchior K.G./Licher Privatbrauerei** in Lich with **LICHER PILSNER PREMIUM** — bright gold, pleasant light hop aroma, zesty hop flavor with plenty of malt in back, a little soapiness in the long malt aftertaste but not enough to be bothersome, and **LICHER DOPPELBOCK PREMIUM** — deep amber, big malt nose, chewy malt flavor, big and bold, very rich, full bodied, very long malt aftertaste, a clean and complex brew with lots of character; **Privat-**

brauerei Eder in Grossostheim with **EDER PILS** — hazy yellow, light hop nose, big hop flavor up front, sour malt in back, fair balance, long dry hop aftertaste, **BAVARIA BAYERISCH WEIZEN** — gold, lactic spicy malt nose, clean wheat taste with only the faintest lactic spice, clean wheat and malt finish and aftertaste, **EDER PRIVAT EXPORT** —hazy gold, grainy molasses nose, big body, big malt flavor, long and rich, ends dry malt, **EDER DOPPELBOCK DUNKEL** — deep ruby-brown, big toasted malt nose, big creamy rich malt flavor, finely carbonated, huge body, very long and very satisfying, **BAVARIA DUNKLER STARKBIER** — deep amber, lovely toasted malt nose, big malt flavor, rich and delicious, a heavy malt beer with lots of alcohol, long malt aftertaste continues to show the alcohol, and **BAVARIA BAYERISCH MÄRZEN DUNKEL** — deep amber-gold, lovely malt nose, big dry roasted malt flavor, very drinkable, dry malt aftertaste has a caramel nature but is quite dry.

Where Were They?

As we travelled about the countryside scouring supermarkets, gas stations, and getränktmarkts, buying up every new beer we could find, some of those that turned up defied our efforts to locate. The label gave the name of the beer, the brewery and the town of origin. The only problem was that the best maps that we could find there (and in libraries here at home afterwards) did not include these towns. I know that some of these towns like Gnodstadt, Böbrach, and Adlersberg (that we did find) are missing from all but the most detailed maps. The breweries in the towns below exist, but I do not yet know where to find the towns. They may be very small towns, or be suburbs of cities not normally named separately. In any event, here they are.

Schlossbrauerei Haselbach in Haselbach with **D'WIRTSDIRN SCHWARZE DUNKLES HEFEWEISSBIER** — brown, big thick head, malt aroma has a spicy background, flavor is more roasted malt than spice (which is way in back), big tasty flavor, very smooth long malt aftertaste, with the spiciness still hiding far in back.

Schlossbrauerei Irlbach in Irlbach with **IRLBACHER VOLLBIER HELL** — gold, pleasant malt and hop nose, smooth balanced flavor, long dry hop aftertaste, a good long refreshing brew; **IRLBACHER PILS** — gold, nice hop and malt nose, balanced, mostly hop flavor, long dry hop aftertaste, good body; **IRLBACHER SCHLOSSHERRN WEISSE** — deep brown, thick head, light lactic-malt nose, flavor to match, medium long dry malt aftertaste, very drinkable; and **IRLBACHER ECHT BAYERISCHES HEFE-WEIZEN** — hazy gold, light spicy malt nose and taste, good balance, dry malt finish and aftertaste.

Rhanerbräu in Rhan with **RHANER EXPORT HELL** — gold, hop nose, malt flavor, good balance and body, off-dry malt finish and aftertaste.

Privatbrauerei Adolf Schmid in Usterbach with **REISCHENAU GOLD HELLES EXPORT** — gold, hop nose, malt flavor, fine hops in back, finish and long aftertaste are more malt than hops, good body, good balance, a fine beer; **USTERBACHER PILSNER** — gold, hop nose, big hop flavor with plenty of support from the malt, dry hop finish, very well-balanced, long dry malt and hop aftertaste; and **USTER-BACHER BAYERISCH HEFE-WEIZEN** — cloudy gold, big spicy malt nose and taste, plenty of cloves and cinnamon, good finish like the flavor leading into a long dry malt and hop aftertaste with a spicy background.

Fürstlicher Brauerei Schloss Wächtersbacher in Wächtersbach with **WÄCHTERSBACHER JUBILAUMSBIER 400 PREMIUM** — tawny-gold, roasted malt nose, malt flavor, nutty candy finish, long somewhat dull malt aftertaste, lacks zest; and **WÄCHTERSBACHER FÜRSTEN PILS CLASSIC** — pale gold, faint malt nose, dry malt palate, bone dry finish, fairly long dry malt aftertaste. (Believed to be from area northwest of Frankfurt.)

Brauerei Distelhäuser in Distelhausen with **DISTELHÄUSER PREMIUM PILS** — gold, hop nose and flavor, long dry hop aftertaste, good body, but just hops; **DISTELHÄUSER EXPORT** — gold, malt nose and flavor, good body, dry hop finish, long dry hop aftertaste; and **DISTELHÄUSER MÄRZEN** — gold, malt nose, strong malt flavor, good balance, good body, long dry hop and malt aftertaste.

Privatbrauerei Beck in Trabelsdorf with **BECK UNSER DUNKLES** — brown, toasted malt nose, light toasted malt flavor, medium body, dry toasted malt finish and aftertaste, not long.

We also found a few stragglers from northern Germany and I include them here for completeness. Most of them are either a special type of beer, a well-known beer for quality or come in an unusual bottle, or have an unusual label or name.

Privatbrauerei Karl Hintz in Marne i Holstein with **DITHS-MARSCHER MAIBOCK** — copper-amber, rich malt nose and zesty malt flavor, big body, long malt aftertaste, very rich and very good, and **DITHSMARSCHER UR-BOCK** — deep bright reddish copper, light malt aroma, big malt flavor, plenty of hops for balance, rich and big bodied, very long malt and hop aftertaste.

Hübsch & Koch brewery in Bohlendamm, Hannover with **PUPASCH DUNKEL** — amber, pleasant malt and hop nose, light toasted malt flavor, tasty and pleasant, light dry malt aftertaste, a flavorful easy drinking beer.

Privatbrauerei Gambrinus Nagold of Hamburg with **BÖLK STOFF** — gold, tangy hop and malt aroma, strong malt and big bright hop flavor, zesty and mouth-filling, complex and strong, very long dry hop and malt aftertaste, good strong sipping beer that lasts and lasts.

Brauerei Gatzweilers in Dusseldorf with **GATZWEILERS ALT** — medium brown, sour hop nose and front palate, dry hop middle and finish, dry hop aftertaste with some sour malt in back, medium body, medium length.

Gilden Brauerei of Köln with **GILDEN KÖLSCH** — gold, light hop and malt aroma and flavor, smooth and balanced, light body, long aftertaste like the flavor.

Hannen Brauerei, Gmbh. in Monchengladbach with **HANNEN ALT** — deep tawny-gold, sour cardboard nose, burnt cardboard taste, thin body, dull aftertaste.

Privatbrauerei Diebel in Issum/Wiederrhein markets **DIEBEL'S ALT** — brown, tangy ale-like nose, smooth zesty malt flavor with good hops in back, dry malt finish and long dry malt aftertaste, there is a spicy ale-like tang in the background all the way across the palate and through the aftertaste as well.

Aachener Burgerbauerei/ Peter Wiertz Gmbh. in Aachen with **BURGERBRÄU PILS** — gold, faint malt and hop aroma, dull malt flavor with some hops in back, dull malt finish, short dry malt aftertaste.

Felsenkeller Brauerei in Monschau issues **ZWICKELBIER HEFETRUB-DUNKEL** — hazy amber, pleasant malt aroma, very dry malt flavor, light body, short dry malt aftertaste.

Brauerei Emil Petersen Gmbh. & Co., K.G. in Flensburg with **FLENSBURGER PILSENER** — pale gold, pleasant light fresh malt aroma, malt palate with a flash of bitter hops in the middle that stay into a long dry bitter hop aftertaste.

A Month Is Not Enough

As we travelled throughout the land, we knew that it could not all be done in a month. Some things had to be missed to see others. I'm not just referring to those places where we would have liked to spend more time, for there are many of those, but I'm thinking of those places we missed entirely. We missed out on the Staatsbrauerei in Freising because of weather. We would have enjoyed a visit to Schloss Kaltenburg, Weltenburg Monastery, and the last three remaining *Klosterbrauereien* that still have monks and nuns brewing beer. One of these is in Mallersdorf on the road between Landshut and Regensburg. Another is in Furth, on a picturesque back road between Landshut and Mainburg. The other is in Ursberg, north of Augsburg. There are also many other klosterbrauereien that we did not reach on our tour. These are the ones, like Ettal and Andechs, where brewing operation is no longer in the hands of clerics, but where marvelous beer is still made according to the old recipes.

There are also many, many more Hausbrauerei (or brewpubs) and Privater *Brauereigasthöfe* (that's the plural) that are available for lodgings. In addition to those specified previously, there are these additional places *that I know of* in Southern Germany.

BRAUEREI GASTHOF GROSCH in Rödental (6 km from Coburg)
GASTHOF SCHNUPP in Altdrossenfeld (near Kulmbach)
BRAUEREI GASTHOF DREI KRONEN in Memmelsdorf (near Bamberg)
ZUM STIEFEL in Saarbrucken
BRAUEREI SCHIESSL in Amberg
WINKLER BRÄUSTÜBERL in Lengenfeld
     (between Nürnberg and Regensburjg)
HOTEL HÄFFNER BRÄU in Bad Rappenau
BRAUEREI GASTHOF WINKLER in Berching
     (between Nürnberg and Regensburg)
BRAUHAUS GASTSÄTTE FAM. MÜLLER in Gunzenhausen (near Nürnberg)
BRAUEREIGASTHOF KAMM in Zenting (between Regensburg and Passau)
BRAUEREIGASTHOF ST. GEORGE in Hemau/Neukirchen (near Regensburg)
GASTHOF GOLDENER HAHN in Belingries
     (between Nürnberg and Ingolstadt)
SCHLOSSBRÄUSTÜBERL ODELZHAUSEN in Odelzhausen
     (between Augsburg and Munich)
BRÄU IM MOOS in Tüssling (half way between Munich and Passau).
     I do not believe them to have rooms.
ZUM ADLER in Moosbeuren (near Ulm)
HOTEL LÖWENBRÄU in Bad Wörishofen (between Augsburg and Kempten)
BRAUEREI HOTEL HIRSCH in Ottobeuren (near Memmingen)
HOTEL POST in Nesselwang (20 km from Füssen)
CAFE SCHÖNECK in Heidelberg
VOGEL BREWPUB in Karlsruhe
MAHR'S BREWERY TAVERN in Wunderberg (near Bamberg)
GOLDENER STERN HOTEL in Ebersdorf (between Bamberg and Coburg)
WACKER BRAUEREI HOTEL in Gauerstadt (near Rodach and Coburg)
DREI KRONEN TAVERN in Strassgeich (near Bamberg)
DER HAUSBRAUER DIETZ GASTHOF in Bruckberg (Near Nürnberg)
SCHLOSSBRÄU-KELLER AU HALLERTAU in Hallertau
     (near Freising)

Just to remind you, all of the above are breweries as well as restaurants, hotels, etc. They will average two or three beers each and those are available, for the most part, only on premises or within a 2-3 mile radius. You have to go there to taste them.

I will go back again and again. I will revisit those places that have given me so much pleasure. I will go to new places where I expect to be met with new tastes, sights and excitement. Give Germany your attention and you will be amply rewarded. It is a beautiful country with marvelous people and great beer.

Index